Judaism's Great Debates

The Jewish Publication Society
expresses its gratitude for
the generosity of the following
sponsors of this book:

PATRONS:
David Lerman
and Shelley Wallock

FRIENDS:
D. Walter Cohen
Wendy and Leonard Cooper
Rabbi Howard Gorin
Gittel and Alan Hilibrand
Marjorie and Jeffrey Major
Jeanette Lerman Neubauer
and Joe Neubauer
Gayle and David Smith
Harriet and Donald Young

UNIVERSITY OF NEBRASKA PRESS

LINCOLN

JUDAISM'S GREAT DEBATES

Timeless Controversies from Abraham to Herzl

RABBI BARRY L. SCHWARTZ

THE JEWISH PUBLICATION SOCIETY
PHILADELPHIA

Manufactured in the United
States of America

Library of Congress
Cataloging-in-Publication Data
Schwartz, Barry L.
Judaism's great debates : timeless
controversies from Abraham to Herzl /
Barry L. Schwartz.
p. cm.
"Published by the University
of Nebraska Press as a Jewish
Publication Society book."
Includes bibliographical references.
ISBN 978-0-8276-1131-3 (pbk.: alk. paper)
1. Judaism—History. 2. Religious dispu-
tations. 3. Judaism—Doctrines. I. Title.
BM157.S39 2012
296.3—dc23 2011046028

Set in Minion and Perpetua
by Kim Essman.
Designed by Nathan Putens.

Contents

Acknowledgments

Great appreciation is owed to my wife, Debby, my children, Nadav, Talia, and Noam, and my parents, Barbara and Rudy, for their unending support during tumultuous times; to my students of all ages, who studied and debated this material with me; and to The Jewish Publication Society and Behrman House, two great publishers who have cooperated to make this book available in both adult and student textbook editions.

Sincere and heartfelt thanks to David Lerman and Carol Hupping of The Jewish Publication Society, David Behrman and Mark Levine of Behrman House, Donna Shear of the University of Nebraska Press, and Edmond Weiss.

Translations of biblical texts are from NJPS TANAKH, The Jewish Publication Society's 1985 English translation of the Hebrew Bible. Translations of Rabbinic texts are generally mine, unless otherwise noted. The actual debate texts consist of direct quotes (in italics) together with my re-created dialogue (regular print).

— *Rabbi Barry L. Schwartz*

Introduction

Arguing for the Sake of Heaven

"Every debate that is for the sake of heaven
will make a lasting contribution.
Every debate that is not for the sake of heaven
will not make a lasting contribution."
TALMUD, AVOT 5:20

Judaism not only maintains a great respect for debate; one could read-ily argue that debate is central to its religious expression.

According to the Torah, Abraham is involved in a great debate . . . with God. Moses has a serious argument with his own cousin. Five daughters of a deceased Israelite challenge their tribal leaders. King David is confronted by one of his closest advisors.

The Talmud is replete with debate. Indeed, it coins an important expression: *makhloket l'shem shamayim* (an argument for the sake of heaven), which remains a key tenant of Jewish thinking. Our sages understood that a debate for the right reasons enhances Judaism. A debate for the wrong reasons detracts from Judaism.

The importance and worthiness of a good debate is illustrated in a well-known passage about the students of the famous rabbis Hillel and Shammai:

For three years there was a dispute between Beit Hillel and Beit Sham-
mai, the former asserting, the law is in agreement with our views, and

*the latter contending the law is in agreement with our views. Then a
voice from heaven announced: eilu v'eilu divrei elohim hayim, both
are the words of the living God . . . but the law is in agreement with
the ruling of Beit Hillel.* (Talmud, Eruvin 13b)

The first of two crucial points that emerge from this critical teaching is
the deep respect for differing opinions. Hillel and Shammai represent
two opposing schools of thought. Throughout the Talmud, these sages
and their students can be found sparring with each other. Yet "both
are the words of the living God," because both sides are speaking the
truth as they see it, and have the welfare of the community in mind.

The second crucial point is the courage to act. Respect for differing
viewpoints did not inhibit the sages from deciding important matters.
A majority ruled in favor of Beit Hillel, and that became the law. Our
ancestors rallied around these communal decisions time and again.
The followers of Shammai were not necessarily happy that in this
instance (and most of the time) Beit Hillel (the House of Hillel) won
and Beit Shammai (the House of Shammai) lost. Yet both the majority
and minority understood that everybody won, in the sense that the
debate was fair and the decision-making process honorable.

The esteemed nineteenth-century German rabbi Samson Raphael
Hirsch sums up the value of worthy debate:

> *When in a controversy both parties are guided by pure motives and
> seek noble ends . . . and when both parties seek solely to find the truth,
> then, of course . . . only one of the two opposing views can and will
> prevail in practice.*
>
> *But actually, both views will have permanent value because, through
> the arguments each side has presented, both parties will have served to
> shed new light on the issue under debate, and will have contributed to
> the attainment of the proper understanding of the question discussed.*
>
> *They shall be remembered as . . . advancing the cause of the genuine
> knowledge of truth.*[1]

The value bestowed upon worthy debate is affirmed in similar fashion,
but with a mystical bent, in the teaching of a famed Hasidic sage.

Rabbi Nachman of Bratslav explains that debate is a holy form of communication. The holiness is derived from the way debate echoes the divine process of *tzimtzum,* making space for the creation of something new. Just as God entered into an act of self-limitation in order to make possible the created world, so debaters restrain themselves in order to make room for opposing viewpoints. As Rabbi Or Rose comments on the Bratslaver:

> *When we disagree with one another, when we take sides, we create the necessary space for the emergence of new and unexpected ideas. Without makhloket . . . the horizon of human discovery would be severely limited.*[2]

Debate is more than a valued intellectual exercise in Judaism. In echoing the divine process of creation, it is a holy act.

EVEN GOD LOVES A GOOD DEBATE

A classic talmudic story involves a debate between Rabbi Eliezer ben Hyrcanus and several of his fellow sages. The specific topic of the debate is not earth shattering: whether the oven of a man named Aknai is considered ritually clean or not. While the tale is recorded in folkloric terms that are often fanciful and humorous, the larger issue of who has the right to decide *halakhah* (traditional Jewish law) is indeed weighty:

> *It has been taught: On that day Rabbi Eliezer brought forward every imaginable argument [that the oven was ritually clean], but the sages did not accept them.*
>
> *Rabbi Eliezer said to them: "If the halakhah agrees with me, let this carob tree prove it!" Thereupon the carob tree was torn a hundred cubits out of its place — others say four hundred cubits.*
>
> *"No proof can be brought from a carob tree," the sages replied.*
>
> *Again he said to them: "If the halakhah agrees with me, let this stream of water prove it!" Whereupon the stream of water flowed backward.*

"No proof can be brought from a stream of water," they replied.

Again he said to them: "If the halakhah agrees with me, let the walls of this schoolhouse prove it!" Whereupon the walls of the schoolhouse inclined toward falling.

But Rabbi Joshua rebuked all of them saying: "When scholars are engaged in a debate of Jewish law, what right have you to interfere?"

So the walls did not fall, in honor of Rabbi Joshua, nor did they resume the upright position, in honor of Rabbi Eliezer. They are still standing tilted.

Again he said to them: "If the halakhah agrees with me, let it be proved from Heaven!"

Whereupon a voice from Heaven cried out: "Why do you debate with Rabbi Eliezer, seeing that the halakhah agrees with him every time?"

Rabbi Joshua then arose and exclaimed: "The answer is not from Heaven!"

The debate concludes on the defiant note of Rabbi Joshua that not even God has the right to interfere in a rabbinic debate on a matter of religious law!

Yet this is not quite the end of the story. One of the sages goes on explain that the Torah itself gives people the right to debate and decide matters of Jewish law by majority vote. The rabbi cites a verse from Exodus (23:2) with the expression *"follow the majority"* to prove the matter. A close look at the original context of the quote doesn't necessarily prove anything. This almost seems to be beside the point, however, when one considers the remarkable continuation of the text:

What did the Holy One, blessed be He, do in that hour [after the debate]? God laughed [with joy] and replied, "My sons have defeated Me, My sons have defeated Me!" (Talmud Baba Matzia 59b)

Our sages intended this tale as a powerful affirmation of our right to think and argue for ourselves. The story's addendum goes even further by suggesting that God loves and honors a good debate. We may interpret these dramatic words as additional testimony to the rabbinic concept of debate as holy act.

And even here the story is not finished, as is so often the case in the Talmud. A disquieting denouement, rarely cited, is tacked on to the narrative. The postscript is itself open to debate, but in the minds of most interpreters it is understood to affirm the central point.

According to the text, Rabbi Eliezer is harshly disciplined by his fellow sages for his dissent from the majority, and is excommunicated by his peers. The esteemed Rabbi Akiva is sent to deliver the edict as humanely as possible. Yet Rabbi Eliezer is personally devastated. A series of natural calamities ensues, afflicting all the community, in apparent punishment to the sages for rebuking their colleague and his right to dissent. Even Rabbi Gamliel, head of the Sanhedrin and Eliezer's own brother-in-law, is struck down and eventually dies for his role in the matter.

The tragic denouement, so different in tone from the main story, is apparently a cautionary postscript about the consequences of intolerance. The sages did not take kindly to the legitimate but incessant dissent of one of their own and tried to stifle it. They should have known better. As Rabbi Clifford Librach understands the morale of the story: *"Woe to those who squelch or discipline the articulation of nonconformity. . . . Dissent is the blood of Judaism."*[3]

JUDAISM'S GREAT DEBATES

Great debates in Judaism continued long past the days of the Torah and Talmud. The preeminent sage of the medieval era, Maimonides, was contradicted by another giant of the times, Nachmanides. The legendary founder of Hasidic Judaism, the Baal Shem Tov, was castigated by the leading jurist of the day, the Vilna Gaon. Baruch Spinoza engaged in a dramatic argument with the leaders of his community in Amsterdam and was excommunicated. In the 19th century new expressions of Judaism, Reform and Conservative, arose amid strident debate. Even Theodor Herzl's attempt to establish a new homeland for the Jewish people in Israel was met with severe ideological opposition.

Echoes of the great debates in Judaism resound in our world today.

Religion tackles the big questions in life; the great debates wrestle with what we believe and how we act. This book presents ten debates, by no means exhaustive of all the great controversies, but largely representative of three categories of concern: political (how we govern), ethical (how we decide what is right), and spiritual (how we understand God and religion).

Judaism as a religion has been inseparable from the Jewish people and the Land of Israel. For significant parts of its history Judaism has wrestled with questions related to national sovereignty, such as: *Who should be in charge?* (chapter 1), *To fight the enemy or accommodate?* (chapter 5), *To rebuild a Jewish state or not?* (chapter 10). These questions remain of interest to Jews who are both citizens of modern Israel and of democracies that solicit their participation.

Questions of morality and ethical action are central to Jewish debate from its beginning. These questions may emerge in biblical times, from Abraham: *Should we listen to our conscience?* (chapter 1), to the Prophets: *Is the leader always right?* (chapter 4), to a dispute among the Twelve Tribes: *Should women have equal rights?* (chapter 3). Yet all these questions continue to be debated today.

Spiritual and ritual questions have likewise been central to Jewish debate through the ages: *Who should determine Jewish law?* (chapter 6), *What are the boundaries of Judaism?* (chapter 8), *Does Judaism change and evolve?* (chapter 9), *Should I engage my mind or heart?* (chapter 7).

When assessing the significance of these debates I have found it useful to carefully consider three issues: *context, content,* and *continuity.*

CONTEXT: Each of these debates arises within a specific set of historical circumstances, and each involves unique personalities. At the beginning of every chapter I attempt to convey the basic historical backdrop so that we can fully understand the ensuing debate. Who is debating, and why? I add a touch of bibliographic background to identify the personalities involved in the debates.

CONTENT: I preserve the debate, whenever possible, by using the actual words of the debaters, gleaned from primary sources. However, I employ poetic license to fill in the gaps, indicated by a change in typeface. In some cases we know that the debaters never met in person, but rather conducted their debate through correspondence or among disciples. For dramatic effect I recreate the debate as a direct confrontation.

From our study of history and psychology we realize that communication often conveys more than one level of meaning at a time. An argument may have an explicit agenda as well as a hidden, or deeper, purpose. When analyzing debates I have found it worthwhile to pose two questions: What is this debate about? What is this debate *really* about? Examining how the verdict of the debate addresses these two questions gives us a greater appreciation of its significance.

CONTINUITY: Each of these debates was important in its time. Most had an immediate impact that altered the course of events in their day. The determination of their ultimate significance, however, (and why I consider them great debates) is how they echo throughout Jewish history. In the last section of each chapter I consider each debate's legacy.

The subject of debate is dear to my heart. In high school, my primary extracurricular activity was tournament debate. In college and seminary I gained an appreciation of rabbinical debate in the classical sources of Judaism. As I was writing this book, and teaching its chapters to adults and youth, people instantly warmed to the subject and often exclaimed, "Of course, Judaism is all about debate." Yes, indeed it is!

Judaism's Great Debates

PART 1
Biblical Judaism

1

Abraham and God

"Where's Your Conscience?"
The First Jewish Debate over Justice

Will You sweep away the innocent along with the guilty?
Shall not the Judge of all the earth deal justly?
ABRAHAM, GENESIS 18:22, 25

THE ENIGMA OF ABRAHAM

We call him *Avraham Avinu,* Abraham our Father. He is venerated by the three monotheistic religions of Western Civilization — Judaism, Christianity and Islam — as the spiritual father of their faith. He is chosen (or chooses) to undertake an epic journey in response to the terms of a covenant with God. That covenant promises progeny, land, and blessing.

Yet there is little in the biblical text to indicate that Abraham will challenge so boldly the God who commands his life so thoroughly. In response to the call to *"Go forth from your native land and from your father's house"* (Genesis 12:1), Abraham, with seemingly no hesitation, uproots home and family and *"went forth as the Lord commanded him"* (Genesis 12:4). He continues each step of his momentous journey with minimal reaction, perhaps in response to continued expressions of divine reassurance. He accepts God's directive to circumcise himself and all the males in his household, no questions asked. Most astonishingly, Abraham submits to God's excruciating command to sacrifice his beloved son Isaac with nary a word of objection.

3

So it comes as something of a shock that the patriarch of unquestioning faith steps forward to challenge God when he learns of the divine intention to destroy the wicked cities of Sodom and Gomorrah:

> *Now the Lord said, "Shall I hide from Abraham what I am about to do . . . ? Then the Lord said, "The outrage of Sodom and Gomorrah is so great, and their sin so grave. I will go down to see whether they have acted according to the outcry that has come to Me; if not, I will take note."* (Genesis 18:17–21)

Then quite suddenly *"Abraham came forward"* (Genesis 18:23) and dares God to morally justify the collective punishment of the innocent with the guilty!

The Great Debate

Here is the debate between Abraham and God as portrayed in Genesis 18:22–32:

ABRAHAM: *Will You sweep away the innocent along with the guilty? What if there should be fifty innocent within the city: will You then wipe out the place and not forgive it for the sake of the innocent fifty who are in it? Far be it from you to do such a thing, to bring death upon the innocent as well as the guilty, so that innocent and guilty fare alike. Far be it from You! Shall not the Judge of all the earth deal justly?*

GOD: *If I find within the city of Sodom fifty innocent ones, I will forgive the whole place for their sake.*

ABRAHAM: *Here I venture to speak to my Lord, I who am but dust and ashes: What if the fifty innocent should lack five? Will you destroy the whole city for want of the five?*

GOD: *I will not destroy if I find forty-five there.*

ABRAHAM: *What if forty should be found there?*

GOD: *I will not do it, for the sake of the forty.*

ABRAHAM: *Let not my Lord be angry if I go on: What if thirty should be found there?*

GOD: *I will not do it if I find thirty there.*

ABRAHAM: *I venture again to speak to my Lord: What if twenty should be found there?*

GOD?: *I will not destroy it, for the sake of the twenty.*

ABRAHAM: *Let not my Lord be angry if I speak but this last time: What if ten should be found there?*

GOD: *I will not destroy, for the sake of the ten.*

GOD AND THE ETHICS OF COLLECTIVE PUNISHMENT

Abraham's dramatic dialogue with God is all the more remarkable for the moral challenge that frames the entire conversation. Abraham's bold pursuit of justice before God is posed right at the outset, with the piercing question: *"Will you sweep away the innocent with the guilty?"* Before God can even reply Abraham proceeds to answer the question! In good debate fashion Abraham seeks to define the terms of the dispute. He assumes as a given that God acts according to a moral code that distinguishes between innocent and guilty, with only the latter punished for their acts. Abraham moves right on to the question of how many innocent people would allow the city of Sodom to be spared.

The fact that God enters into and continues the dialogue with Abraham on his terms seems to indicate that God accepts Abraham's argument that it is wrong to punish the innocent with the guilty. But the question remains: how many innocent individuals would it take to spare an entire city? With every deferential question (another wise tactic against a more powerful opponent) Abraham lowers the number. For some reason, Abraham stops arguing at ten innocent people.

Even though the debate appears to be cut short, Abraham has made his point. Yet tragically, soon after the debate the Torah records that cities of Sodom and Gomorrah were destroyed. Did God uphold the terms of the debate? Were less than ten innocent people to be found? If Abraham's intention was to save the cities from destruction he failed. If his intention was to give God pause, to make God think twice as it were, he may have succeeded.

This debate, then, ends in questions. The abrupt and truncated conclusion shifts the enigma of Abraham to the enigma of God: *"When the Lord had finished speaking to Abraham, He departed; and Abraham returned to his place"* (Genesis 18:33). Does the judge of all the earth in fact act justly?

THE CALL OF CONSCIENCE

Some years ago there was a popular television commercial that featured an individual about to evade moral responsibility, but then a voice calls out, "This is your conscience, Joe."

The debate between Abraham and God, on a deeper level, is about the importance of speaking up and challenging authority when your conscience calls. Abraham was clearly disturbed by what God revealed to him. To its credit, the Torah establishes through this debate that for the sake of justice even God can be questioned.

Abraham could easily have chosen to look the other way. Instead he decides to take a stand against God, who is at once both a formidable opponent and his guide and protector. In the process of doing so, Abraham exemplifies a great commandment that appears later in the Torah, the responsibility to take action in the face of injustice: "*Do not stand idly by the blood of your neighbor*" (Leviticus 19:16).

In the words of psychologist and Torah teacher Naomi Rosenblatt, this story is about *"the power of one man of integrity to be the conscience of the world."* Abraham's conscience does not allow him to keep silent. His tone is respectful, but his questioning is unrelenting. Abraham did not know the people he was trying to save. He is not even arguing that the majority are innocent or that their sins are forgivable. Rather, he is questioning a rush to judgment that may rob individual human beings of their right to just treatment.

Some commentators have seen this debate as yet another in a series of tests of Abraham's character. God chooses to disclose His own intentions to Abraham in order to see how Abraham responds. In this regard, Abraham wins because he came to the defense of the innocent even as he loses the fight to save the cities. Abraham passes the character test by standing his moral ground while maintaining his relationship with his creator. In the words of Holocaust survivor and Nobel Prize–winning humanitarian Elie Wiesel:

To be a Jew means to serve God by espousing man's cause, to plead for man while recognizing his need of God. And to opt for the Creator

*and His creation, refusing to pit one against the other. Of course
man must interrogate God, as did Abraham; articulate his anger,
as did Moses; shout his sorrow, as did Job. But only the Jew opts for
Abraham-who-questions and for God-who-is-questioned. . . . Only the
Jew knows that he may oppose God as long as he does so in defense
of His creation.*[1]

ABRAHAM'S LEGACY: HOLY HUTZPAH

Abraham's bold challenge of God for the sake of justice was the first
Jewish debate. Generations would look back at the founder of the
Jewish people and follow his example. If Abraham argued, so should
we. If Abraham had the courage to challenge God, so should we. If
Abraham stood up for justice, so should we.

The Talmud coined an expression for challenging God in the spirit
of Abraham: *hutzpah k'lapei shemaya* (boldness, or nerviness, against
heaven). A glimpse of this attitude is seen in Moses, who defends
his people against the excesses of God's wrath and warns God not to
endanger His reputation. This "holy hutzpah" is especially evident in
the prayers and stories of the Eastern European Hasidic tradition. Two
remarkable examples come from Rabbi Levi Yitzhak of Berditchev.

In the first, the Rebbe, although deferential like Abraham, is ready
to litigate against God to end the suffering and exile of the Jewish
people:

> *I come to You with a lawsuit from Your people Israel.*
> *What do you want of your people Israel?*
> *From my stand I will not waver,*
> *And from my place I shall not move*
> *Until there be an end to this Exile.*
> *Yisgadal v'yiskadash shmei raboh —*
> *Magnified and sanctified is only Thy name.*

In the second example a story is told of a simple tailor who argues
with God on Yom Kippur. The tailor exclaims:

You wish me to repent of my sins but I have committed only minor offenses. I may have kept leftover cloth, or I may have eaten in a non-Jewish home, where I worked, without washing my hands. But you O Lord have committed grievous sins. You have taken away babies from their mothers and mothers from their babies. Let us be even. You forgive me, and I will forgive You.

Rabbi Levi Yitzhak replied: *"Why did you let God off so easily? You might have forced God to save all of Israel!"*[2]

THE HAUNTING QUESTIONS

The legacy of Judaism's first great debate is both the challenge to God and to our own conscience. Abraham compels us to confront the call of conscience in general and the dilemma of collective punishment in particular. An otherwise obedient and passive Abraham may have been roused to action by the enormity of the injustice that he feared would be perpetrated on a civilian population.

The most excruciating example of collective punishment in our time is the dropping of the atomic bomb on Japan in the hope of ending the Second World War. A brief description in a New Orleans museum of the U.S. bombing expresses the dimension of the dilemma:

On March 9–10, 1945, bombs incinerated 16 square miles and killed 100,000 civilians. In April, bombs destroyed 180 square miles, killed 300,000 people, and left 8.5 million people homeless. Throughout the war, the United Sates resisted bombing civilian areas. But with time, attitudes hardened. What once was unthinkable became a deliberate policy.[3]

The issue of noncombatant immunity and proportionality, subsets of the ethical issue of collective punishment during wartime, continue to bedevil armies and governments. The bombing of Hiroshima and Nagasaki elicit emotional and disparate reactions to this day. Even the wording of museum descriptions and historical texts, such as the example cited above, have been the subject of public controversy. The atomic bombings caused horrific death and damage. And yet many veterans in particular argue that the bombings, by forcing the surrender of Japan and forestalling a ground invasion of that country, saved perhaps a million allied soldiers' lives.

In an age when terrorists hide behind the cover of civilian populations the issue has taken on new aspects. For example, Israel is regularly accused of using disproportionate means of defense, even as it is the subject of repeated attacks. The distinction between civilian and soldier is even subject to debate: at what point does aiding and abetting terrorists change the status of a bystander?

Abraham's questions, *"Will you sweep away the innocent along with guilty?"* and *"Shall not the Judge of all the earth deal justly?"* continue to haunt us.

2

Moses and Korah

Who Is Holy?
The Debate over Holiness and Authority

For all the community are holy, all of them, and the Lord is in their midst.
Why then do you raise yourselves above the Lord's congregation?
KORAH TO MOSES, NUMBERS 16:3

MOSES AND KORAH: COUSINS IN CONFLICT

An argument can be made for considering Moses among the preeminent leaders in history. As the political and moral leader of the Israelite slaves in Egypt he bequeathed to Western civilization fundamental notions of both freedom and responsibility. The improbable Exodus is viewed as the paradigmatic example of resistance to tyranny and the God given right to choose one's destiny. The Revelation at Mount Sinai is the foundation of the Judeo-Christian moral code that informs our ethical sensibility.

As real as his accomplishment, Moses is a mythic figure. His very existence has no independent confirmation outside the Bible itself. Yet the Torah portrait of Moses is remarkably sophisticated and nuanced. Scripture does not shy away from describing Moses's grandeur or his fallibility. Moses's accomplishments are monumental; his failures epic. Moses's willful authority will foster resentment and rebellion; his anger will trigger tragedy and denial of his dream to lead his people into the Promised Land.

One would not expect, however, that a severe challenge to his leadership would come from within his own family and tribe. Yet the Book of Numbers recounts just such a course of events. Korah, a Levite leader, is a cousin to Moses; their fathers, Amram and Izhar, are brothers. He is joined in his challenge by three other prominent leaders named Dathan, Abiram and Og, and eventually by 250 other tribal *"chieftains of the community, chosen in the assembly, men of repute"* (Numbers 16:2). The Torah makes clear, then, that this is no mere family squabble. The instigator is Moses's own blood relative, but the challenge engulfs the entire community.

The challenge to Moses needs to be understood against the backdrop of a long desert trek that has grown increasingly arduous and divisive for the beleaguered Israelites. The triumphant Exodus and awe-inspiring Revelation are already distant memories. Survival in the harsh terrain is increasingly perilous; food and water are in chronic short supply. The people cannot live on promises alone, and dissension grows.

Twelve spies, one from each tribe, are sent to scout out the Promised Land. They return with the majority deeply pessimistic. Only Joshua and Caleb have faith that the Israelites can succeed in overcoming the well fortified inhabitants to enter Canaan. The response of the people that ensues is the most serious to date:

> *The whole community broke into loud cries, and the people wept that night. All the Israelites railed against Moses and Aaron. "If only we had died in the land of Egypt," the whole community shouted at them, "or if only we might die in this wilderness!" Why is the Lord taking us to that land to fall by the sword? Our wives and children will be carried off! It would be better for us to go back to Egypt! And they said to one another, "Let us head back for Egypt."* (Numbers 14:14)

On the heels of this disaster, Korah and his allies launch their challenge against Moses and Aaron.

The Great Debate

Here is the debate between Korah and Moses (and two other rebels), based on Numbers 16:1–16. (Note: italics are direct quotes from the Torah; regular print is added dialogue.)

KORAH: *You have gone too far! For all the community are holy, all of them, and the Lord is in their midst. Why then do you raise yourselves above the Lord's congregation?*

MOSES: *Come morning, the Lord will make known who is His and who is holy, and will grant him access to Himself. God will grant access to the one He has chosen.*

KORAH: You think you are the only chosen one. We are too.

MOSES: *The man whom the Lord chooses, he shall be the holy one. You have gone too far, sons of Levi!*

KORAH: I am from your tribe and am fit to lead just like you and your brother.

MOSES: *Hear me, sons of Levi. Is it not enough for you that the God of Israel has set you apart from the community of Israel and given you access to Him, to perform the duties of the Lord's Tabernacle and to minister to the community and serve them?*

KORAH: No it is not enough. The people need to hear my voice now.

MOSES: *God has advanced you and all your fellow Levites with you; yet you seek the priesthood too! Truly, it is against the Lord that you and all your company have banded together.*

Dathan and Abiram: *Is it not enough that you brought us from a land flowing with milk and honey to have us die in the wilderness? Shall you lord it over us?*

MOSES: God has chosen me to lead. Keep the faith, like Joshua and Caleb.

DATHAN AND ABIRAM: We shall all die here following you. Now God chooses us.

MOSES: *Tomorrow, you and all your company appear before the Lord, you and they and Aaron.* Then we shall see who God chooses.

THE NATURE OF HOLINESS

Korah publically challenges his exalted cousin: "What makes you so special? What makes you so holy? What gives you the right to lord it over us? *For all the community are holy.*"

The Torah speaks of holiness in connection to time, space, and people. The Sabbath and festivals are designated holy days of rest and celebration unlike any other. Mount Sinai and Jerusalem are among select places that are called holy. When describing people as holy the Torah most often speaks in the collective sense, rather than about the individual.

The Book of Exodus notably exhorts, "*You shall be to Me a kingdom of priests and a holy nation*" (19:6). The Book Leviticus famously commands (in the plural), "*You shall be holy, for I the Lord your God am holy*" (19:2). The Book of Numbers (in the paragraph just before the beginning of the Korah incident), explains the importance of the fringed garment known as the *tallit* by stating, "*Thus you shall be reminded to observe all My commandments and to be holy to your God*" (15:40).

As the esteemed Israeli philosopher Yeshayahu Leibowitz astutely notes, a running debate courses through Judaism as to whether holiness is acquired or intrinsic. Those who believe the former tend to argue that we become holy based on our attempts to follow divinely given instruction. Those who believe the latter tend to argue that we are inherently holy by virtue of being created in God's image. Leibowitz explains these dual notions of holiness with a clear bias toward the former:

> *The [first concept] of holiness is not a fact, but a goal.*
>
> *In the [second concept] holiness is something granted to us; we are holy.*
>
> *The difference between the two is most profound. On the one hand holiness is expressed as the most lofty state that can be attained through*

man's decisions on religious faith; he is required to demand this goal of himself. On the other hand we have holiness[in which] a person absolves himself of responsibility, of the mission imposed upon him and of the obligation to exert himself; he is smugly sure that he is already holy. And we have been aware of this at all times — that even the most contemptible person can boast that he is a member of a holy nation. But one should note, without distorting the fact, that in the long history of Judaism, these two concepts of holiness have existed side by side.[1]

Korah clearly belongs to the second school of holiness. All are holy, he argues, so no one, not even Moses, should exercise absolute power over another. Moses places himself in the first camp when he insists that we are holy when God says we are. God presumably designates us as holy when we have earned that distinction. Accordingly, Moses claims it is fitting that certain people are chosen to rule over others.

Leibowitz echoes the thought of the great German Jewish philosopher Martin Buber, who wrote:

Both Moses and Korah desired the people to be . . . the holy people. But for Moses this was the goal. In order to reach it, generation after generation has to choose again and again . . . between the way of God and the wrong paths of their own hearts. . . . For Korah, the people . . . were already holy . . . so why should there be further need for choice? Their dispute was between two approaches to faith and to life.[2]

In the same vein Rabbi Shlomo Riskin, a prominent Orthodox leader, highlights the seductive appeal of Korah's view:

The conflict between Moses and Korah reflects a tug of war within the human spirit . . . Korah denies the importance of the laws. He says, "Who needs this system of do's and don'ts, you shalls and you shall nots. We're holy already." Certainly this perspective was attractive to every Israelite who wanted to be left alone. Who wants to be told what to do and what not to do?[3]

In their negative assessment of Korah all three of these thinkers offer an ideological component to the harsh judgment of Moses' cousin leveled by tradition. According to the Torah, there was no question about who was in the right and who was in the wrong in this debate. Korah and his followers are considered rebels. They meet the terrible fate of being swallowed up alive:

Scarcely had he [Moses] finished speaking all these words when the ground under them burst asunder, and the earth opened its mouth and swallowed them up with their households, all Korah's people and all their possessions. (Numbers 16:31–32)

KORAH'S LEGACY: POPULIST OR DEMAGOGUE?

The harsh critique of Jewish tradition generally concentrates not so much on ideology, however, but on motivation. Korah represents an obvious challenge to Moses' authority. Almost all the rabbinic commentary doubts Korah's motive and integrity. The sages claim that the debate was just an excuse to attack Moses for personal gain. In their view, Korah did not have the welfare of the community in mind, but only his own lust for power.

In fact, when the Talmud distinguishes between worthy debates ("for the sake of heaven") and unworthy debates ("not for the sake of heaven"), the example given of the latter is none other than the one we are discussing:

And what debate was not for the sake of heaven? Such was the debate of Korah and all his followers. (Avot 5:17)

Korah earns the dubious distinction of forever being the exemplar of dishonest dispute. His message is undermined by his motive. In this view, no matter what the content of his critique, Korah was wrong. According to Rabbi Harold Schulweis:

The lesson of Korah, then, is not that dissent must be squashed but that the character of the dissent and its motivations be sincere. Korah's dissent was manipulative and his intent self-serving. Where the dissent is moral, honest and without ulterior motive, it is the will of God.[4]

Few commentators have been willing to deviate from this indictment of Korah and wrestle with his actual message. But there are some commentators who make the claim that Korah's message should not be negated by his motives. They argue that while his power grab was illegitimate, his critique was not. For instance, Bible teacher Evan Wolkenstein offers:

Like all good revolutionaries, [Korah's] uprising has some legitimacy. Korah claims that the whole nation is holy and should therefore have access to power. This is, after all, a time-honored articulation of populism.[5]

Rabbi Bradley Artson, a noted author and rabbinic leader, elaborates on this theme:

Korah's challenge strikes to the heart of democratic values. . . . If all people are created equal, then, why should any one person have any authority over another? Why should one person ever have access to power, wealth, or prestige in a way that another person does not? . . . each person has intrinsic worth . . . all people have equal value.[6]

History teaches us that there is a fine line between populism and demagoguery. Korah seems to have crossed that line. Yet upon dispassionate reflection, Korah may offer a legitimate albeit alternative view of the nature of holiness with implications for the way we choose and regard leaders. Unfortunately his impure motivations preclude any serious discussion of his argument in the rabbinic sources.

HOLY DEBATABLE

The question of acquired vs. inherent sanctity is more significant than one might think. The issue is not confined to esoteric religious discussion. It is also of real consequence spiritually and even politically. Previously I mentioned that the Jewish concept of *kedusha,* holiness, extends to time, space, and people. Let us consider an example from each category.

TIME: Is the Sabbath inherently holy? Or is the day rendered special by our actions? What then constitutes appropriate observance of the Sabbath? How does one interpret the biblical prohibition of work on this day? Should Israel, the Jewish State, mandate certain Sabbath policies for all its citizens?

SPACE: Is Jerusalem an inherently holy city, and the Western Wall the most sacred site in Judaism? Or are Jerusalem and the Wall special because of their history? Should Israel relinquish or share sovereignty over holy cities and sites?

Comparison to an American analogy is thought provoking. Independence Hall in Philadelphia is considered by many to be an example of a sacred site. Most would argue that the Hall acquired sanctity by virtue of its role as the birth place of the nation; the site where the Declaration of Independence and Constitution were signed. Not far away, President Abraham Lincoln declared Gettysburg hallowed ground. Sanctity is ascribed due to the heroic nature of the sacrifice made there, but perhaps too from the legacy of the great leader and his magnificent tribute.

PEOPLE: Are the Jews inherently holy as the Chosen People? Or are they distinguished by their self chosen mission, or their long and unique history? Are certain leaders the elect of God?

Inherent notions of sanctity usually posit God as the source of holiness that is beyond human determination. Many traditional Jews accept on faith that God promised a particular land to a particular people, and may choose certain leaders. Moses and Korah may even have been in general agreement on this thesis. Yet their dispute on the implications of holiness opens up a wider and more consequential debate than they could have imagined.

3

The Five Daughters and the Twelve Tribes

Equal Rights?
The Debate over Inclusion

The plea of Zelophehad's daughters is just . . .
The plea of the Josephite tribe is just.
MOSES TO THE ISRAELITES, NUMBERS 27:7, 36:5

WHEN SISTERS STAND UP

The five sisters are hardly household names, even to people who know their Bible. Mahlah, Noah, Hoglah, Milcha, Tirzah are the unmarried daughters of an Israelite man of the tribe of Manassah named Zelophehad, who dies in the desert with no male heirs. In a brief but significant encounter recorded in the Book of Numbers, these young women seek inheritance rights from their tribe.

At this early point in the evolution of Jewish law, the Torah provides that only males inherit and pass down property and possessions from one generation to the next. The five daughters of Zelophehad note the unfortunate circumstance of their father's passing without male progeny, and that both his wealth and his legacy will unfairly be taken from his family. The sisters' appeal to Moses and the tribal leaders is heartfelt and poignant:

Our father died in the wilderness. He was not one of the factions, Korah's faction, which banded together against the Lord, but died for his own sin; and he has left no sons. Let not our father's name be lost to his clan just because he had no son! Give us a holding among our father's kinsmen! (Numbers 27:3–4)

These brave sisters seek nothing less than a change in tribal law. Moses, either sympathetic or simply confounded, seeks divine guidance. God's response is swift and affirmative regarding the change (Numbers 27: 6–11). The Torah narrative then moves on to other matters, only to belatedly revisit the issue when the tribal leaders object (Numbers 36:1–12). In the following account of the debate I conflate the two chapters to sharpen the exchange.

The Great Debate

Here is the debate between the daughters of Zelophehad and the tribal leaders, with responses from God and Moses, based on Numbers 27:1 — 11 and 36:1–12. (Note: italics are direct quotes from the Torah; regular print is added dialogue).

DAUGHTERS: *Our father died in the wilderness . . . and he has left no sons. Let not our father's name be lost to his clan just because he had no son. Give us a holding among our father's kinsmen.*

MOSES: Your request, though respectful and understandable, is new. I must think about this and determine God's will.

GOD (TO MOSES): *The plea of Zelophehad's daughter is just; you should give them a hereditary holding among their father's kinsmen; transfer their father's share to them.*

MOSES: We understand your situation, and will allow you to inherit your father's possessions.

DAUGHTERS: You honor our father's memory.

GOD (TO MOSES): *Further, speak to the Israelite people as follows: If a man dies without leaving a son; you shall transfer his property to his daughter.*

MOSES: So shall I proclaim the law to the tribal leaders.

TRIBAL LEADERS: *God has commanded to assign the share of our kinsman Zelophehad to his daughters. Now, if they marry persons from another Israelite tribe, their share will be cut off from our ancestral portion and be added to the portion of the tribe into which they marry. Thus our allotted portion will be diminished.*

MOSES: I understand this problem, because the law states that when a woman marries outside her tribe, she becomes part of his household, and her rights are transferred to his. Again, I will determine God's will in this matter.

TRIBAL LEADERS: We seek only fairness and justice for our tribes.

MOSES: *The plea of the Josephite tribe is just. This is what the Lord has commanded concerning the daughters of Zelophehad: They may marry anyone they wish, provided they marry into a clan of their father's tribe. No inheritance of the Israelites may pass over from one tribe to another, but the Israelites must remain bound each to the ancestral portion of his tribe. Every daughter among the Israelite tribes who inherits a share must marry someone from a clan of her father's tribe, in order that every Israelite may keep his ancestral share.*

THE POLITICS OF INCLUSION

The debate in the Torah about inheritance rights for women was bound to arise. The possibility of a man dying without any sons is not remote. Biblical law seems to have overlooked the situation until the five daughters raise the matter. God's immediate and affirmative verdict might be seen as an example of the judicial system attempting to correct itself.

Upon close examination this change does not grant women regular inheritance rights. It is limited to the case where no male heirs exist. A legal complication arises, which the tribal leaders raise with Moses. Biblical women were entitled to marry men from outside their tribe, and when they married, any inheritance rights are transferred to their husbands. So in effect, a marriage of any of the five sisters would diminish the holdings of their tribe. The family would gain at the expense of the tribe.

The tribes (or at least their male leaders) strenuously object to this prospect. Moses (and God) is quick to see the merit of the tribal argument. He expresses the justness of their concern as he had previously done for the daughters.

What should be done when both sides of a debate are right? Obviously, some type of compromise is in order. Moses, again said to be acting according to divine instruction, orders just such a thing. Women will be able to inherit if there are no male heirs, but they will be required to marry within the tribe.

Interestingly, the Book of Joshua goes out of its way to relate that Moses's decision was fulfilled after his death, once the Israelites actually settled in the Promised Land: *"So in accordance with the Lord's instructions, [the daughters] were granted a portion among their father's kinsmen"* (Numbers 17:4). From the Torah's point of view, the compromise seems to be a win/win situation for family and tribe.

The daughters of Zelophehad seemed to be pleased by the compromise that allowed them to inherit property while requiring them to marry within the tribe. Judged by the standards of their time, the sisters won a significant victory in the battle for equality. These sisters are consistently praised in rabbinic literature as courageous and wise.

Yet judged by the standards of today the sisters won only a partial victory. This case does not grant women the right to inherit under normal circumstances. An important restriction is put on who they can marry. One can even argue that the women did not win true inheritance rights, but merely the ability to be a place holder until the next generation of male heirs could take over.

The daughters' debate over an inheritance issue was more for the sake of their family than themselves. It led to an important correction to inheritance law that elevated the status of women in one circumstance. But it did not change the overall inequality of biblical law. As Rabbi W. Gunther Plaut observes:

> *While the Torah records a number of laws in which men and women are treated equally, it is on the whole male-oriented. The male has rights the female does not enjoy. She is to be wife and mother, invested with inherent dignity, to be sure, but by law and social order relegated to a second-class status.*[1]

THE DAUGHTERS' LEGACY: SEPARATE BUT EQUAL?

Traditional Jewish law *(halakhah)* defines a separate status for women. Women are not allowed to serves as rabbis, cantors, judges, or witnesses. They are not counted in a *minyan* (ten men required for communal worship), cannot lead a public worship service, read from the Torah, or be called to the Torah for an *aliyah*. Historically, few women filled positions of leadership in the community, and they were given considerably less education than men.

One rationale often cited for these restrictions in the law is the desire to exempt women from time-bound commandments that would take them away from the home. By extension, a person who is not required to perform certain duties is therefore not eligible to be a leader of those activities. So, for example, a woman who is not required to be part of a public prayer service cannot represent the community as a leader of such prayer.

Another rationale is tied to the perception that women can be a distraction to men. In traditional prayer and celebratory settings males sit apart from females for this reason. The female voice is judged inappropriate for public singing because of its potential to arouse men.

Defenders of the tradition argue that all this represents a separate-but-equal status for women in Judaism. Opponents argue for the need for radical change that corrects unacceptable inequality. Such change has occurred in the non-Orthodox denominations of Judaism, and only in the last few decades.

The groundwork for the dramatic move toward equality was laid by the early Reform movement in Germany. Already in 1837, Rabbi Abraham Geiger, one of Reform's pioneers, argued:

> *Let there be from now on no distinction between duties for men and women . . . no assumption of the spiritual inferiority of women, as though she were incapable of grasping the deep things in religion; no institution of the public service, either in form or content which shuts the doors of the temple in the face of women.*

Only nine years later at an important gathering of Reform rabbis called the Breslau Conference, the group declared that *"it is a sacred duty to express most emphatically the complete religious equality of the female sex."*[2]

In 1922 Judith Eisenstein celebrated the first modern bat mitzvah. In 1972 Sally Priesand was ordained as the first female rabbi. Today the majority of new cantors in the Reform, Reconstructionist and Conservative movements are female and the percent of new rabbis is split nearly evenly between men and women. Synagogue presidents and board members are as likely to be female as male.

The debate over inclusion now occupies a prominent place of discussion in modern Jewish life. On a wider scale, this debate has expanded from equal rights for women to the status of many minorities and nontraditional members of the Jewish community. The role of gays and lesbians is one prominent example; the status of interfaith couples is another.

When I began rabbinical school more than a quarter century ago, women had recently won the previously unthinkable right to be ordained as rabbis. But a classmate of mine who was gay had to conceal his sexual orientation in order to be ordained. Today that is no longer the case in the non-Orthodox movements. At that time, commitment ceremonies for people of the same sex were unheard of. Today Reform rabbis can decide the matter for themselves. Fully equal marriage ceremonies for homosexuals and lesbians remain a subject of intense controversy not only within Judaism, but in our society at large.

Interfaith marriage is viewed by many in the Jewish community as both contrary to Jewish law and a threat to Jewish survival. Others see it as another challenge on the frontier of true inclusion. The debate over rabbis officiating at such marriages is considerable; so too the role of the non-Jewish partners in synagogue life.

The Torah itself contains passages proscribing homosexual behavior and interfaith marriage. At the same time it repeatedly teaches us to embrace the marginalized and powerless in society. The well-known verse, *"You shall not oppress a stranger, for you know the feelings of the strangers, having yourself been strangers in the land of Egypt"* (Exodus 23:9) is mentioned in one form or another thirty-six times in the Torah. Expanding the circle of inclusion and bestowing equal rights for all is a centuries old effort in our country and a millennia old struggle in Judaism. We've come a long way from the five sisters to Rabbi Sally Priesand. Not every one agrees with the magnitude of change that is beyond the wildest dreams of the biblical women. Yet the changes, and the debate about them, will continue.

4

David and Nathan

Does Might Make Right?
The Debate over Accountability and Morality

And Nathan said to David, "That man is you!"

2 SAMUEL 11:7

King David, ancient Israel's greatest monarch, came from humble origins. He grew up a shepherd to his family's flocks in Bethlehem. While still a boy he comes to notice in an unlikely victory over a giant Philistine warrior named Goliath. The Bible, our sole biographical source, relates that David is chosen by God, and anointed by Samuel, as the second King of Israel, when Saul fails at his task.

David's rise to power is the longest single narrative in the Hebrew Bible. The passionate and charismatic monarch secures the safety of Israel and greatly enlarges its borders. He makes Jerusalem the capital and in a grand ceremony brings the Holy Ark of the Covenant there. David enjoys a remarkably long and prosperous reign. Yet he is beset by personal problems. It is said that David can rule a kingdom but not his family.

Nathan is a confidante and advisor to the king. More significantly, he is a prophet; one of those self-anointed individuals who claim to communicate God's will. The prophets trace their inspiration back to Moses, who enjoyed a uniquely close relationship to the divine.

Nathan, and Samuel, who is both a judge and prophet, are the first in a long line of men who will speak "truth to power." Fearless in their faith, the prophets confront kings and countrymen alike when they deem it necessary.

David is at the height of his powers when he has an affair with a woman named Bathsheba. He spies the woman bathing from his roof, summons her to the palace, and lies with her despite learning that she is married. Bathsheba becomes pregnant from the encounter.

Having already committed adultery, one of the Torah's most grievous sins, David complicates the matter by conspiring to conceal the affair. He brings Bathsheba's husband, Uriah, back from battle with the hope that he will sleep with his wife. Ever the good soldier, Uriah stays with the troops, even when intoxicated. The King of Israel escalates his error by then plotting to have Uriah sent to the front lines and killed in battle. Adultery has now been compounded by murder. After the period of mourning, David marries Bathsheba, who bears a son from their adulterous union.

"But the Lord was displeased with what David had done, and the Lord sent Nathan to David" (2 Samuel 12:1). Nathan learns of the affair and cover-up. As close as he is to the king, he is first and foremost a prophet in God's service. Nathan's confrontation with King David is epic. Yet it begins in the most curious way . . . with a story.

The Great Debate

Here is the famous dialogue between King David and the prophet Nathan, based on 2 Samuel 11–12. (Note: italics are direct quotes from the Torah; regular print is added dialogue).

NATHAN: Let me tell you a true story.

DAVID: I am listening.

NATHAN: *There were two men in the same city, one rich and one poor. The rich man had very large flocks and herds, but the poor man had only one little lamb. He cared for it and it grew up with him and his children . . . One day, a traveler came to the rich man. But the rich man did not want to take anything from his own flock to feed the guest.* So he stole the poor man's lamb instead.

DAVID: That is outrageous. *The man who did this deserves to die! And he should pay for the lamb four times over, since he stole it and showed no pity.*

NATHAN: *That man is you!*

DAVID: What are you talking about? I am the king!

NATHAN: *Thus says the Lord, the God of Israel: It was I who anointed you king over Israel . . . and gave you everything you have. Why then have you flouted the command of the Lord and done what displeases him? You have put Uriah to the sword; you took his wife and made her your wife and had him killed.*

DAVID: You are right; I cannot deny it.

NATHAN: God will punish you. *The sword shall never depart from your house. I will make a calamity rise against you from within your own house. You acted in secret, but God will make this happen in the sight of all Israel and in broad daylight.*

DAVID: *I stand guilty before the Lord.*

NATHAN: *You shall not die. But the child about to be born to you shall die.*

NO ONE ABOVE THE LAW

The confrontation between prophet and king is not so much a debate about morality as accountability. To convey his message that even the King of Israel is accountable before God (never mind his people), Nathan must first capture the monarch's attention. Nathan begins by telling David a simple story. When David reacts strongly to the parable of a rich man stealing from a poor man, exclaiming that the sinner deserves to be severely punished, Nathan springs the rhetorical trap: That man is you!

David apparently doesn't think that his wrongdoings were right, but he did think that he could get away with these crimes because he is king. When directly confronted with his sins, David immediately admits his guilt. After all, he has broken two of the Ten Commandments: adultery and murder, not to mention the lying and deceit associated with the cover-up.

Perhaps David's guilty conscience will not permit him to remain in denial before the prophet. Perhaps he genuinely fears God's wrath. In his prophetic role Nathan proclaims that David, given his confession and remorse, will be allowed to continue serving as king. But the king will pay a heavy price. *"The sword shall never depart from your house . . . the child about to be borne to you shall die"* (2 Samuel 12:10, 13). Indeed, the biblical narrative continues with an emotional account of the David's reaction to the death of his child. The very next chapter relates the rape of David's daughter Tamar by her half—brother, Amnon. Her full brother, Absalom, plots Amnon's death in revenge for the violation of his sister. The sword of domestic mayhem strikes David before his very eyes.

If the prophet Samuel had been still alive at this time, he might have said, "I told you so." When Samuel first anointed Saul he did so

reluctantly, warning the people that kings would try to place themselves above the law.

> *This will be the practice of the king who will rule over you: He will
> take your sons. . . . He will take your daughters . . . He will seize your
> fields . . . He will take your flocks . . . The day will come when you cry
> out because of the king whom you yourselves have chosen; and the
> Lord will not answer you on that day.* (1 Samuel 8:11–18)

This warning about the excesses of royalty is already embedded
in Deuteronomy, where the tribes are cautioned about appointing a
king who will abuse his power: *"He shall not keep many horses . . . He
shall not have many wives, lest his heart go astray; nor shall he amass
silver and gold to excess"* (2 Samuel 17:16–17). In a powerful symbolic
reminder that no one, not even the king, is above the law, the Torah
goes on to require that the monarch keep a copy of the Torah by his
side at all times:

> *Let it remain with him and let him read it all his life, so that he may
> learn to revere the Lord his God, to observe faithfully every word
> of this teaching as well as these laws. Thus he will not act haughtily
> toward his fellows or deviate from the Instructions to the right or to
> the left, to the end that he and his descendants may reign long in the
> midst of Israel.* (2 Samuel 17:19–20)

So the story of Nathan before David is the remarkable tale of a prophet
who prevails over the most powerful king of Israel at the height of his
powers. David thought he could (literally) get away with murder, not
to mention adultery. Did David come to believe that as God's anointed
he was above the law, or could avoid its consequences? Nathan knew
better. He knew that he must confront the king, at the risk of his
friendship, status, and maybe even life. Nathan was ultimately loyal
to God, and when his friendship with David was put to the test, he
had but one choice.

In the long run, the people of Israel gain by this show of prophetic
courage. The confrontation establishes clear limits on the power of
the monarchy. Even kings are responsible to uphold Torah law.

This story also hints at the power of repentance. By quickly and decisively acknowledging his guilt David saves his kingship and maybe his life. David will pay a terrible personal price; the repentance involves sacrifice and suffering. An emotionally troubled king will continue to prosper politically. And while David and Bathsheba lose their baby, they go on to have another son, named Solomon. It is none other than Solomon who will become the next king, who will build the great Temple in Jerusalem, and who will gain renown as a wise, law abiding, and successful monarch.

THE PROPHETIC LEGACY: TRUTH TO POWER

The figure of the prophet in ancient Israel is unprecedented and unique. These men, with no armies or political power of their own, confront kings and generals. They are armed with only their moral authority. Nathan's encounter with David inspired generations of prophets. Elijah confronts Ahab; Isaiah confronts Hezekiah, and Jeremiah confronts Zedekiah. The prophets speak truth to power.

The prophets were equal-opportunity gadflies; they clashed with kings and countrymen alike. They railed against idolatrous belief and false piety. They admonished the rich for injustice and apathy toward the poor. They cautioned against foreign alliances that undermined true faith. Yet they so believed in the power of repentance that they also offered inspirational messages of hope in times of trial.

The legacy of the prophets is especially seen in movements for social justice driven by religious leaders. The civil rights struggle in the United States is an illuminating example. Martin Luther King Jr. made frequent reference to the prophets. He urged Americans to protest unjust segregation laws by practicing the kind of lofty rhetoric and confrontational but non-violent civil disobedience that the prophets would have approved of. The rabbis who marched with Dr. King were similarly inspired by the prophets. One of them, Rabbi Joachim Prinz, was chosen to speak at the 1963 March on Washington just before King's unforgettable "I Have A Dream" speech.

Another rabbinic activist and ally of Dr. King was the renowned teacher and thinker Rabbi Abraham Joshua Heschel. In a 1973 interview Heschel explained that his study of the prophets changed his life:

I've written a book on the prophets. A rather large book. I spent many years. And really, this book changed my life. Because early in my life, my great love was for learning, studying. And the place where I preferred to live was my study with books and writing and thinking.

I've learned from the prophets that I have to be involved in the affairs of man, in the affairs of suffering man.

The great examples we need today are the ancient prophets of Israel.

And I think that anyone who reads the prophets will discover, number one, that the prophets were the most disturbing people who ever lived. Abrasive, disturbing, giving me a bad conscience.

[The prophets] combine a very deep love, a very powerful dissent, painful rebuke, with unwavering hope.[1]

PART 2

Rabbinic Judaism

5

Ben Zakkai and the Zealots

Brains or Brawn?
The Debate over Resistance

My children, why do you destroy this city
and why do you seek to burn the Temple?
YOCHANAN BEN ZAKKAI, AVOT D'RABBI NATAN 4:5

A HOUSE DIVIDED

On the eve of the greatest calamity in ancient Jewish history, the destruction of the Second Temple and the fall of Jerusalem, one family produced two leaders with polar opposite approaches to the conflict with Rome. An uncle and his nephew rose to prominence in radically different circles. Rabbi Yochanan Ben Zakkai was the greatest sage of his generation, and a pivotal figure in Jewish history. His nephew, called Abba Sikra, whose real name may have been Ben Batiah, was a rebel leader who remains among the most shadowy and controversial figures of the Second Temple period. In a supreme irony, Abba Sikra will play a key role in not only opposing his uncle, but in eventually saving his uncle's life and legacy.

Rabbi Yochanan ben Zakkai (ca. 30–90 CE), a disciple of the renowned Hillel, is a figure of major importance in the Talmud and Midrash, which record his life in a blend of fact and legend. He is a leading authority on the interpretation of Scripture and Jewish law. As a sage he is part of a movement of Rabbinic leaders, the Pharisees, who are often at odds with the Sadducees, the priests who serve the

Temple. These internal disputes among the religious leadership centered primarily on ritual and theological matters.

But as Roman occupation and rule, now more a century long, grows increasingly harsh, there is no escaping political involvement and division. Rabbi Yochanan gains a reputation as an advocate for accommodation, arguing for cooperation with Rome in order to carry on daily life as normally as possible. He urges maintaining peace *"between nation and nation, between government and government, between family and family"* (Mekhilta, Ba-Hodesh, 11). He warns that rebellion against Rome is futile and will only bring more misery and destruction upon the people.

Abba Sikra, son of Rabbi Yochanan's sister, could not disagree more. He and his fellow zealots hold that the yoke of Rome must be thrown off at all costs. They argue that the fight for freedom must continue no matter the degree of suffering. In their zeal they even resort to attacking fellow Jews who disagree with them, accusing them of collaboration with the enemy. The daggers they carried are called *sicari;* their faction adopts that name; and Yochanan's nephew Abba Sikra ("father of the assassins") is their militant head.

The Great Debate

Here is the debate between Ben Zakkai and Abba Sikra of the Zealots, based on stories recounted in the Gittin 56a-b, Avot d'Rabbi Natan 4:5, Lamentations Rabbah 1:5 and Ecclesiastes Rabbah 7:12. (Note: this is a reconstructed conversation between uncle and nephew, although actual statements from the above texts are incorporated; italics are direct quotes from the sources; regular print is added dialogue).

ABBA SIKRA: As you have heard, I commanded that the storehouses of Jerusalem be burnt. We must fight the Romans at all costs. If it takes starving our countrymen to make them fight, so be it.

BEN ZAKKAI: *Woe!*

ABBA SIKRA: *Why do you make that exclamation?*

BEN ZAKKAI: *Because so long as the stores were intact the people would not expose themselves to the dangers of battle.* Now that you are starving them, they will be become desperate, and they will fight.

ABBA SIKRA: That is exactly what we intend.

BEN ZAKKAI: *My children, why do you destroy this city and why do you seek to burn the Temple?* For that is exactly what Vespasian will do to us if you rise up against him.

ABBA SIKRA: We bow only to God; not to a Roman, be he a general or an emperor.

BEN ZAKKAI: *What is it that Vespasian asks of you? In truth he asks nothing of you save one bow or one arrow, and then he will leave you alone.* The tribute tax he requires is a small price to pay.

ABBA SIKRA: *Even as we went forth against the two generals before him and slew them, so we shall go forth against him and slay him.*

BEN ZAKKAI: You are making a terrible mistake, and the people will suffer. *Be not in haste to pull down the high places of the gentiles, lest you have to rebuild them with your own hand. It is written that thou shall build the altar of unhewn stones, and shall lift up no iron tools upon them. If these stones are meant to make peace between Israel and God, then they are also meant to make peace between man and wife, family and family, city and city, nation and nation, and between government and government.*

TWO WARS: EXTERNAL AND INTERNAL

The debate about resisting Rome divided a family and a nation. Rabbi Yochanan ben Zakkai sided with those who thought the wise thing to do was to appease Rome and not incur the wrath of Vespasian, the general who becomes emperor. When Abba Sikra, who urged throwing off the yoke of a foreign empire by any means necessary, senses his uncle's position prevailing, he takes the desperate step of burning Jerusalem's storehouses to inflame the situation and force the people into action. In the hope of igniting external war against Rome Abba Sikra stokes the fire of civil war, pitting Jew against Jew, brother against brother.

The debate, then, is not only about how to deal with the Romans, but also how to deal with one's fellow citizens. Each side claims it has the nation's best interest in mind. Yet each side emphasizes different values and therefore different courses of action. Ben Zakkai thought that military action would only lead to destruction and defeat. He preached an accommodation that would enable the country to survive. As a sage, he urged the people to put their energy into religious observance, not revolt. Abba Sikra, by contrast, believed so strongly in the need to fight that he and his fellow zealots were willing to force his fellow citizens to take up arms whether they wanted to or not. The zealots intimidated and bullied the population into accepting their views.

This is not the first time that ancient Israel had faced the question of how to respond to an invading power. The Maccabees dealt with the situation of the occupying Greeks in similar fashion. Their campaign against the Seleucids was accompanied by a ruthless drive against fellow Jews who collaborated with the Greeks. While the festival of Hanukkah celebrates their external victory against a superior army, the details of their civil war are only known through a close reading of the Book of Maccabees (ironically, included not in the Hebrew Bible but the Christian canon).

Perhaps Abba Sikra and the zealots were hoping for another miracle.

But this time there would be no happy ending. Rabbi Yochanan's deepest fears would be realized. In the year 70 CE, the Temple is destroyed and Jerusalem falls. Three years later the last of the zealots, holed up in the desert fortress at Masada, commit mass suicide rather than surrender. The Jews would not regain sovereignty in their country until two thousand years later.

"GIVE ME YAVNEH"

There is a fascinating postscript to the debate between Rabbi Yochanan ben Zakkai and Abba Sikra, which helps elucidate the legacy of their dispute. When the rabbi determined that Jerusalem was about to be attacked by the Romans, he devised a daring plan to sneak out of the city for a secret meeting with the commanding general Vespasian. Rabbi Yochanan faked his own death, and his nephew arranged for his body to be carried out of the city in a coffin.

According to the famous talmudic story, when the rabbi encounters Vespasian he correctly predicts that the general is about to be named emperor. When that indeed happens, Vespasian replies, *"I am now going, and will send someone to take my place. You can, however, make a request of me and I will grant it. He [Rabbi Yochanan] said to him: Give me Yavneh and its sages"* (Gittin 56b).

Yavneh, a town in the Galilee, became the spiritual center of Israel. At Yavneh the sages debated in their academies. The Sanhedrin, a religious high court, convened at Yavneh to decide matters of Jewish law. Much of the Jerusalem Talmud was completed there. During the long and dark decades of Roman occupation, the light of Jewish learning shone forth from Yavneh.

In this place, too, Rabbi Yochanan ben Zakkai propounded a revolutionary new doctrine of Judaism that enabled it to survive national calamity. The doctrine is expressed in a midrashic account of the sage making a return visit to Jerusalem:

Once when Rabbi Yochanan ben Zakkai was leaving Jerusalem, Rabbi Joshua was walking behind him and saw the Temple in ruins. Rabbi Joshua said, "Woe is us that this has been destroyed, the place where atonement was made for the sins of Israel." "No, my son, do you not know that we have a means of making atonement that is like it? And what is it? It is deeds of loving kindness, as it is said [Hosea 6:6]: For I desire kindness, and not sacrifice." (Avot d'Rabbi Natan 4:21)

Reaching back and retrieving a strand of prophetic thought, Rabbi Yochanan ben Zakkai began crafting a new theology that moved Judaism away from its dependence on Temple sacrifice as the means for ritual atonement. Ethics became the new imperative and now *"shulchano shel adam m'caper alav* (one's table atones)." Home is the new homeland; one's table the new altar. This new paradigm introduces the viability of Diaspora Judaism. The process of adapting to the loss of land and sovereignty has begun.

BRAINS OR BRAWN?

Rabbi Yochanan ben Zakkai's vision is powerful testimony to the will and creativity of Judaism to survive tyranny and tragedy through accommodation and adaptability. Yet the debate about resistance, while dormant for periods, never fully dissipated. Indeed the Jews would again rebel against the Romans. A general named Bar Kochba led a revolt in 125 CE and then another in 132 CE Again the populace was divided. The leading rabbi of that generation, Akiva, supported the revolt. And again, the nation was crushed.

The zealots make us think about if and when to use force to resist. They also provoke us to wonder how far we should go in convincing others to join our cause. These twin dilemmas came to the fore again with the creation of the modern State of Israel. In fact, Abba Ahimeir, one of the early militant Zionists who called for violent actions against the British in Palestine, went by the nom de plum "Abba Sikra." In

1930 he founded a faction called "Brit Habiryonim–Covenant of the Rebels," borrowing name from the violent zealots of old.

David Ben Gurion and his moderate Zionist party (the Haganah) urged independence through intense lobbying and other political means. Menachem Begin and his minority militant organization (the Irgun) were more aggressive; they attacked British targets. The most notorious occurred at Jerusalem's King David Hotel, resulting in military and civilian causalities alike.

Although they shared the same goal of independence, the internal dispute over resistance to the British escalated. Eventually Ben Gurion said the Irgun had to be stopped, and he ordered a boat full of Irgun arms to be sunk. Israelis continue to argue about the role of the Irgun and Ben Gurion's decisions, and about the degree to which external threats to Israel's security should be met with negotiation or force. The debate over resistance to evil is alive and well.

6

Hillel and Shammai

Who's the Judge?
The Debate over Jewish Law

Both are the words of the living God . . .
but the law is in agreement with Beit Hillel.
TALMUD: ERUVIN 13B

TWO TEACHERS

Hillel and Shammai. Two names forever paired in Jewish law and lore. Two names synonymous with disagreement and debate. Two names that symbolize mercy and justice, leniency and strictness.

Hillel was *nasi,* head of the Sanhedrin, for forty years. Shammai was his deputy for all that time. Hillel was known for wisdom and compassion. Shammai was known for wisdom and piety. Hillel sought the spirit of the law. Shammai observed the letter of the law. Hillel was beloved of the poor. Shammai was popular with the wealthy.

The two would remain linked long after their deaths. The disciples of Hillel became known as Beit Hillel (House of Hillel). The disciples of Shammai became known as Beit Shammai (House of Shammai). Upon close examination of the Talmud it becomes apparent that Hillel and Shammai, though far different in temperament and style, disagreed on only a handful of legal issues that we are aware of. On the other hand, their disciples disagreed on hundreds of matters, major and minor.

The best-known story about the duo involves the question of how to respond to a person who seeks to convert to Judaism. Several accounts perfectly illustrate their contrasting personalities and manners. The best-known dispute among their students involves the proper way to light Hanukkah candles. The disagreement goes beyond personality, to principle.

Shammai seems to be the ready foil to Hillel in the talmudic record; invariably the majority seems to incline toward the interpretation of Hillel and his school. As the well-known passage in the Talmud (Eruvin 13b) quoted in the introduction of this book declares: *"both are the words of the living God . . . but the law is in agreement with the ruling of Beit Hillel."* The historical record indicates that time and again the majority sided with Beit Hillel, and their interpretation became rabbinic law.

Hillel is deemed one of the greatest sages in Jewish history. His rarified status is reflected in the statement that *"There were four who died at the age of one hundred and twenty: Moses, Hillel the Elder, Rabban Yochanan ben Zakkai and Rabbi Akiva"* (Sifre, Deuteronomy 357). While certainly an exaggeration, the midrashic hyperbole points to Hillel's long life and esteemed tenure as a Rabbinical leader in Israel. Estimates of his birth range from 80–50 BCE., and he likely died in 10 CE As a youth he came from Babylonia to Israel, where he no doubt witnessed the beginning of the Roman occupation of Israel and the controversial efforts of King Herod to win over the Jewish population. Unlike Ben Zakkai and Akiva, we know nothing of Hillel's political involvement.

Hillel's venerable teachings are embedded in the talmudic tractate of Pirkei Avot (Ethics of the Fathers). Among the best known:

Judge not your fellow man until you come into his place. (2:5)

The more Torah, the more life;
the more study, the more wisdom,

the more counsel, the more understanding;
the more charity, the more peace. (2:8)

If I am not for myself, who will be for me?
But if I am only for myself, what am I?
And if not now, when? (1:14)

Hillel's compassionate personality matched his teachings. The same talmudic passage that proclaims his school's interpretation normative goes on to offer a reason why the opinions of Beit Hillel prevailed: *"because the Hillelites were gentle and modest, and studied both their own opinions and the opinions of the other school, and always mentioned the words of the other school with great modesty and humility before their own."*

Hillel's disciples followed their master in personal example. Yet, as their debates with Beit Shammai will reveal, it is their judicial spirit that has lasting consequences for the development of Judaism.

The Great Debate

Here is a debate between Hillel and Shammai, and their students, based on several of the most well-known stories from the Talmud (Shabbat 21b, 31a, Ketubot 16b, Rosh Hashanah 16b–17a). Note: this is an imagined conversation between the two men, and between their students, although actual statements from the above texts are incorporated; italics are direct quotes from the sources; regular print is added dialogue.

SHAMMAI: A gentile came to me the other day and said, *"I will convert to Judaism if you teach me the whole Torah while I stand on one foot."* I told him to get lost and stop wasting my time.

HILLEL: I am sorry you pushed him away. He came to me afterward and I said to him, *"What is hateful to you, do not do to your neighbor. That is the whole Torah; the rest is commentary. Now go and study!"*

BEIT SHAMMAI: We learn from our teacher that you must be strict and honest. *Suppose a bride is lame or blind. Should one say about her, Oh, what a lovely and graceful bride? No, because the Torah warns us against lying. You should describe her as she actually is.*

BEIT HILLEL: We learn from our teacher that you must be lenient and compassionate. *Surely, it is more considerate that praise be spoken at such a time.*

BEIT SHAMMAI: The strict and correct way to light the Hanukkah menorah is this: *On the first day eight candles are let and thereafter they are gradually reduced, by one each day.*

BEIT HILLEL: The way to light the candles that makes the most sense is this: *On the first day one candle is lit and thereafter they are increased each day.*

BEIT SHAMMAI: Our custom is correct because the candles represent the oil, which became less and less. The candles also represent the days of the holiday, which also become less and less.

BEIT HILLEL: We believe our custom is correct because the candles represent the miracle of light, which became greater and greater each day. *One should only increase in matters of holiness and celebration, not decrease.*

BEIT SHAMMAI: The fate of the righteous is heaven; the wicked are condemned to hell, *but those in between shall go down to Gehinnom, and when they tearfully pray they shall come up again.*

BEIT HILLEL: *God inclines the scale of judgment toward mercy;* those in between pray and go directly to the World-to-Come.

JUDICIAL PHILOSOPHY

Beit Hillel and Beit Shammai debated scores of subjects. From the record of these arguments we get a sense of their differing judicial philosophy, the basic assumptions of how to read the law that underlie their approach. We know that the values and approach that a judge brings to a decision greatly influence the judicial conclusion. Even today, when the president nominates someone to the Supreme Court, members of Congress inquire not only about the judge's experience, but also about his or her views of the law.

Hillel and Shammai, and their disciples, did not challenge each other's legal qualifications; all concerned were qualified and experienced. What they did argue about was how strict or lenient a judge should be. Shammai had the more severe personality; and he and his school went "by the book" in his rulings. Hillel possessed a more congenial personality; he and his school were known for flexibility and took many factors into consideration in their rulings.

Shammai brusquely turned away a prospective convert to Judaism, while Hillel welcomed him.

Beit Shammai insisted on telling the strict truth to a bride, while Beit Hillel was more forgiving for the sake of her feelings.

Beit Shammai offered a more logical order on the lighting of Hanukkah candles, while Beit Hillel understood how the ritual would resonate with the people.

Beit Shammai posited a severe view of the World-to-Come, while Beit Hillel expressed a more compassionate and inviting end.

The debates go on and on. The schools of Hillel and Shammai argued about how to recite the prayer, the *Shema* (standing or sitting), the order of the blessings of the *Kiddush* (first the wine and then the day, or vice-versa), the correct knife technique in kosher slaughtering, and the qualifications of witnesses in a court case. Beit Shammai argued that the only acceptable reason for a divorce is if one of the partners in the marriage is proved unfaithful. Beit Hillel argued that there may be many other valid reasons for ending a marriage.

Shammai and his school offered strict and often literal interpretation of Scripture and law. Their view aligns with judicial conservatives today who seek the "original intent" of the United States Constitution. Hillel and his school offered dynamic and sometimes metaphorical interpretation of the same. Their view aligns with judicial progressives who seek the "living spirit" of the law.

MIPNEI TIKKUN OLAM — TO MAKE THE WORLD BETTER

Hillel's innovative approach to the law is evident in his best-known ruling, called the *prosbul* (declaration). Biblical law prohibits payment of interest on loans. The Torah also calls for the cancellation all unpaid loans every seventh year, as a provision of the sabbatical release. While the Torah's intentions may be worthy, their practical effect turned out to be just the opposite. During the Rabbinic period wealthy people increasingly refrained from making any loans at all. They were most afraid that debts could be canceled before their repayment. Indeed, the Torah warns against just this scenario of suspending loans (Deuteronomy 15:9), but it happened nonetheless.

Hillel's bold ruling allows the creditor to collect his debt, even during the sabbatical year, by technically transferring it to the court, which is not subject to the same restrictions as an individual. Shammai and other literalists viewed this as an end-run around the law. Hillel, on the other hand, was determined to address a reality that was hurting the poor, and rendering the rich unworthy. The Mishnah itself explains:

> *This is one of the things that Hillel the Elder instituted, for when he saw that the people refrained from making loans and were transgressing the Torah . . . he established the prosbul."* (Shevi'it 10:3)

Another text comments in similar fashion:

> *Hillel the Elder enacted the prosbul [legal procedure] to make the world better (mipnei tikkun olam) because he saw that people refrained*

from lending money to one another and violated what was written in the Torah, "lest you harbor the base thought." (Sifri, Re'eh 113)

Hillel's progressive approach is clearly an accommodation to reality, and a desire to help the needy. He is willing to broadly legislate to further the spirit of the law. Shammai and his followers (even centuries later) criticized Hillel for this "judicial activism."

Hillel's legacy in opening up Jewish law to interpretation in light of changing circumstances has had monumental impact. The growth of the "second Torah," the oral law *(torah she be'al peh)* to supplement the written law *(torah she b'ktav)* was a giant evolutionary step that permits Judaism to adapt to the radical changes of occupation, loss of national sovereignty, and destruction of the Temple that swept the Jewish people in the decades after Hillel's death. It is no wonder that Hillel and his disciple Rabbi Yochanan ben Zakkai are mentioned in the same breath as Moses.

EILU V'EILU: BOTH ARE THE WORDS

Yet the final word belongs to the contribution of Hillel and Shammai together. Their collective differences in temperament and judicial philosophy influenced Jewish law for the next two thousand years. Rabbis would as a matter of course ask: what is the narrow view, and what is the broad view? Those who ruled from a narrow perspective became know as *machmir* (strict). Those who ruled from a broader perspective became known as *makeil* (lenient).

As Rabbi Joseph Telushkin writes in a recent biography of Hillel:

It says something about Judaism that both Hillel and Shammai, and many of their followers, remain revered figures within traditional Judaism even when they embody opposite approaches to the law and to life itself. In this regard, Talmudic Judaism is anti-fundamentalist. It isn't simply the answer that is prized, it is the argument itself, the culture of disputation, the wrestling with the truth.[1]

Yet Telushkin goes beyond emphasizing Judaism's reverence for a "culture of disputation" to assert that we need both the progressivism of Hillel *and* the conservatism of Shammai:

> *The notion that we sometimes need to read even the words of the Torah with an eye to the metaphorical is a great element of rabbinic Judaism, but surely was also an anxiety provoking one for a group of men trying to hold a culture and a religion together. All the rabbis had to counter the dominance of the Roman Empire was the authority of the Torah and the force of their words. Imagination was needed, but there was always the anxiety that imagination would cross the line, exceed its authority, depart too fully from the literal, and end — as Christianity did — not merely reinterpreting the Hebrew Bible but metaphorizing it out of literal existence and turning it into the foundation of a new faith altogether.*
>
> *This balancing act, between law and story, between legalistic literalism and imaginative freedom, is necessary to keep in mind when thinking about the disputations between the schools of Hillel and Shammai, and also when thinking about Judaism today. Our personal freedoms have never been greater but, in our post-Holocaust, assimilating world, anxiety about continuity has never been higher.*[2]

The *machmir* (strict) versus the *makeil* (lenient) approaches to Jewish law and attitudes are of continuing relevance today regarding the very issues brought to light in the stories of Hillel and Shammai. For instance, in recent times the Jewish community has wrestled with the question of outreach; the degree to which we should welcome and encourage conversion to Judaism and the integration of intermarried couples. Clearly Hillel is more receptive than Shammai, by nature and ideology.

These same stories reveal Hillel defining ethics as the essence of Judaism, and a willingness to shape Jewish law to serve that purpose.

So, for example, today some argue in the spirit of Hillel that the laws of kashrut (dietary laws) need to be revised to reflect higher ethical treatment of animals. Others retort in the spirit of Shammai that it is sufficient to abide by the letter of the law.

Differing judicial philosophy affect almost every issue of *halakhah*. Consider such weighty bioethical issues as abortion and euthanasia. The traditional *machmir* position permits abortion only when the physical health of the mother is endangered. The *makeil* position takes into account the mental health of the mother as well. Termination of medical intervention for a dying individual is subject to a strict timeframe rarely exceeding 48 — 72 hours under a *machmir* view of Jewish law. A *makeil* approach might urge a more expansive approach to defining the meaning of imminent death for the purpose of alleviating suffering.

The debate between conservative and progressive approaches to *halakhah* continues to generate controversy. Not everyone would agree with Telushkin that *"Hillel has long been the Talmud's most famous rabbi. The time has now come to let him become its most influential."* Yet surely all are in agreement with the Hillel's admonition, "Now go and study!" Informed decision making is at heart of all worthy debate.

7

The Vilna Gaon and the Baal Shem Tov

Head or Heart?
The Debate over Spirituality

Whoever lives in joy does his Creator's will.
RABBI ISRAEL BEN ELIEZER

TWO MASTERS

In the mid-eighteenth century, Eastern European Jewry produced two remarkable spiritual masters. They never met, nor even corresponded, yet they engaged in vehement debate through their followers. Like Hillel and Shammai they were fundamentally dissimilar in temperament and outlook. One was the epitome of the establishment; the other a counter-cultural figure. Together they defined the parameters of Ashkenazic spirituality.

The Vilna Gaon (The Genius of Vilna), as he became known, was Rabbi Elijah ben Solomon Zalman (1720–1797). A child prodigy, he was destined to spend his life immersed in the study of Torah and Talmud. As with many of exceeding brilliance, the Vilna Gaon had a reclusive streak and spent most of his life studying alone rather than in the usual *hevruta* pairings that characterized the yeshiva word. The Vilna Gaon moved people through his mind. His commentaries are extremely learned and sophisticated, and emphasize scrupulous analysis and traditional observance. His many followers were motivated by respect, even awe, of his learning.

The Baal Shem Tov (The Master of the Good Name), as he became known, was Rabbi Israel ben Eliezer (1700–1760). Unlike his counterpart's privileged upbringing, the Baal Shem Tov spent his childhood and youth in poverty, likely as an orphan, moving around Poland and the Ukraine. His adult years followed a similar pattern, wandering the countryside as a faith healer, storyteller, and teacher. As he wandered his legend grew as a holy man and even a miracle-maker. The Baal Shem Tov moved people through his heart, as revealed in his fervent praying, singing, dancing, and storytelling.

The followers of the Baal Shem Tov became know as Hasidim (the pious ones). The followers of the Vilna Gaon became know as the Mitnagdim (the opposition). These two groups argued mostly about the nature of our primary religious duty: The Vilna Gaon and the Mitnagdim maintained that study and rigorously following the ritual commandments were our utmost responsibilities. The Baal Shem Tov and the Hasidim argued passionately that prayer and joyous celebration were the true way to draw close to God.

The Great Debate

Here is a debate between the Vilna Gaon and the Baal Shem Tov in the form of an imagined conversation. (Italics represent actual quotes attributed to the two individuals.)

BAAL SHEM TOV: No matter what our circumstances, God is very close. The best way to find God is to pray with complete concentration and joy. *Whoever lives in joy does his Creator's will.*

VILNA GAON: God may be close, but the best way to find God is in studying Torah. Torah is serious business. *Everything that was, is, and will be is included in the Torah.*

BAAL SHEM TOV: Of course, study is important, *but our main purpose is that one should cling to God and attach oneself to the spirit and light of God.* That is best found in prayer, because *the essence of worship is the feeling of oneness with God.*

VILNA GAON: God's plan for us and the world is laid out in the Torah. There in no way to discover God's will other than the regular study of the holy writings.

BAAL SHEM TOV: *Everything created by God contains a spark of holiness.* Everything we do can create a spark. *If you are full of joy, you are full of love.* Singing, dancing, fervent prayer: these express *faith, which is the clinging of the soul to God.*

VILNA GAON: If you lead people away from study, you lead them away from observing the commandments. If you lead them away from the law, they will sin. So what you are doing is itself a sin.

BAAL SHEM TOV: No, I am leading them to joy and love and God.

VILNA GAON: The sages have said, *"Talmud torah k'neged kulam — the study of the law takes precedence over everything."* That is the way it must be. Who are you to say differently?

FINDING GOD

Although the two masters did not meet, one of the myriad of stories told about the Baal Shem Tov involves him engaged in a debate with a naysayer from the Vilna Gaon's school. The opposing rabbi accuses the Baal Shem Tov of being a false prophet, claiming to possess secret knowledge of God and Torah that leads the common person astray. The Hasidic master forcefully denies the accusation and takes the opportunity to explain:

> *What I teach . . . is constantly remembering that God is with you and never letting this thought out of your mind even for a moment.*
>
> *I clearly perceive that the world is directed by divine providence, in even its smallest details.*
>
> *The Torah's sole purpose is to lead a person to faith in the perfect unity, the belief that there is no ultimate reality to anything in existence other than God's essence. Even what appears at first sight to be a separately existing thing is actually completely Godliness, and everything that happens — although it has natural causes or is due to the free choice of human beings — yet its inner cause is divine providence.*[1]

We might call the doctrine that the Baal Shem Tov is espousing "radical immanence." God is everywhere; indeed there is no real existence apart from God. As the Besht (an acronym of his name) adds later in the same debate, "*All places are holy . . . every spoken word is a message from God.*" The consequences of such a worldview are vast. The Besht goes on to criticize most rabbis for wasting time in the pursuit of arcane legal problems rather than spiritual elevation. And in the midst of the debate he is interrupted by a gentile cooper from whom he learns an important lesson.

All this proves too much (at least initially) for the rabbi, who responds:

> *But your belief that even chance conversations are words of Torah,*

that gentiles can be heavenly messengers and their words prophecy, I consider contemptible; for according to your view, holiness can rest on heresy or evil, and the Shekhinah [Divine Presence] *can be revealed even in sinful thoughts. No rational person can tolerate such a view and the Torah totally rejects it. Anyone who accepts this perverted perspective is destined to be punished for it. I certainly can't accept it!* [2]

TWO PATHS

The debate between the Vilna Gaon and the Baal Shem Tov touches on the very essence of religion. Is the quest for God primarily a matter of the head (intellect) or the heart (emotion)? Is faith more about knowledge, or feeling? To be a good Jew, do we have to primarily study, or pray?

The two schools of thought can be summarized as follows:

	Mitnagdim (Vilna Gaon)	**Hasidim (Baal Shem Tov)**
goal	observance	joy
method	study	prayer
approach	*keva* (routine)	*kavanah* (spontaneity)
ideology	rational	mystical
emphasis	*halakhah* (law)	*aggadah* (stories)
result	*de'ah* (knowledge)	*devekut* (closeness)
exemplar	*Hacham* (sage)	*Tzadik* (saint)

Responding to the bleak living conditions of Eastern Europe, the charismatic Besht launched a movement that aimed to restore spiritual joy to the lives of Jews, no matter what the degree of poverty and discrimination they were facing. Many members of the Rabbinical establishment, like the Vilna Gaon, reacted with alarm. They viewed Hasidism as leading Jews astray from their primary responsibilities to study Torah and observe the commandments. For them the secret of the Jews' survival was not in ecstatic celebration but in sober reflection.

In truth, Judaism has taught both immanence (God is near) and transcendence (God is far). The very words of the central High Holy Day prayer offer contrasting images of God: *Aveinu* (Our Father), *Malkeinu* (Our King). In essence one could say that the Besht teaches that one should relate to God like an ever-present parent, while for the Vilna Gaon, one should relate to God like a majestic monarch.

IN SEARCH OF SPIRITUALITY

On a historical basis, the more conservative Mitnagdim prevailed. The vast majority of observant Jews continued to embrace the Rabbinic tradition of intense Torah study and strict adherence to the commandments. The Vilna Gaon and his followers established a network of *yeshivas* (rabbinical academies) that continue to dominate the world of traditional Torah learning to this day.

While the Hasidic movement did grow enough to take root, its numbers remained a distinct minority in the Jewish community. What is more, under pressure from the majority, the Hasidim largely turned from a counterculture movement to an establishment one. The Hasidic world established yeshivas that also emphasized lifelong Torah study, and the Hasidim became so observant that today they are known as "ultra-orthodox." Some Hasidic sects shun contact with the outside world. Others, like the well-known Chabad group, actively engage with the community.

Yet despite their strict and rigorous observances, Hasidic prayer still retains spirited singing, dancing, and storytelling. The Hasidic influence on establishment Judaism helped rekindle the debate over head vs. heart in Judaism in our own day. Some Jews began arguing in the 1960's and 70's that the synagogue world had become too formal, rigid, and spiritually cold. Under the influence of new thinking leaders like Rabbis Shlomo Carlebach and Zalman Schacter-Shalomi (who had both grown up Hasidic and broken away), chanting, meditation, exuberant folk-oriented music, and storytelling began making their way into synagogue services.

Today, folk melodies by composers like the late Debbie Friedman compete with more traditional versions of the prayers, formal sermons vie with discussions, and traditional text-based learning is challenged by experience-based sharing. Interest in Kabbalah (Jewish mysticism) and meditation is strong. Jewish spirituality is again a "hot" topic, but its proper place is still debated.

PART 3
Modern Judaism

8

Spinoza and the Amsterdam Rabbis

Total Freedom?
The Debate over Boundaries

*But having been unable to reform him, but rather, on the
contrary, daily receiving more information about the
abominable heresies which he practiced . . . Spinoza should
be excommunicated and expelled from the people of Israel.*
AMSTERDAM JEWISH COUNCIL

I enter gladly on the path that is opened to me.
SPINOZA

THE DEFIANT SON

Amsterdam in the 17th century was one of the great cities of the
world. An international center of trade and mercantile innovation,
its Protestant rulers also created some of the most tolerant havens
for free thinkers and religious minorities. Amsterdam was home to
artists (such as Rembrandt, who lived in the Jewish quarter), to intel-
lectuals, and not incidentally, to large numbers of Jews who fled the
Inquisition in Spain and Portugal. These Jews had previously lived as
conversos, outwardly Christian but secretly Jewish, and Amsterdam
represented a new opportunity to reclaim their heritage.

Baruch Spinoza (1632–1677) was a son of this Portuguese Jewish
community. He received a traditional Sephardic education and was
evidently an exceptional student. Already as a teen he began to question traditional Judaism, and express radical new ideas.

While Amsterdam was a safe haven for the Jews, the Amsterdam
Jewish Council (Ma'amad) that controlled almost all aspects of Jewish
life was ever-fearful of disturbing the peace. The Council punished

those perceived as troublemakers with fines, and occasionally with banishments that lasted anywhere from a day to a lifetime.

For "abominable heresies" Spinoza was excommunicated in 1656 by the community leaders of the Council at the age of twenty-four. He would never again have any contact with his community or seek readmittance. Spinoza lived alone, and although befriended by Christians and urged to convert, he resisted such overtures. He lived humbly and supported himself as a lens grinder, dying of a heart ailment at only forty-five years of age.

Yet in his lifetime Spinoza earned the reputation as the most brilliant, and controversial, philosopher of his age. He published two major works: *Tractatus Theologico-Politicus* (1670), and *Ethics* (1675). On the strength of the first work alone he was offered a university appointment, which he declined. His impassioned embrace of humanism — rigorous reason, utilitarian ethics, and political tolerance — laid the foundation for much of modern philosophy and government.

The Jewish community of Amsterdam was run by lay leaders (*parnasim*) who actually pronounced the excommunication of Spinoza, but was led by three spiritual heads: Rabbi Saul Levi Morteria (1596–1660), chief rabbi of the community; Rabbi Isaac Aboab (1605–1693), second in command; and Rabbi Manasseh ben Israel (1604–1657), a popular teacher, writer, and pioneering printer. All three may have been Spinoza's teachers. Ben Israel, the freest thinking of the group, was out of the country (in England, attempting to argue to Oliver Cromwell for the readmittance of the Jews) at the time of the excommunication. While the Rabbis disagreed among themselves on some religious matters, especially the acceptability of kabalistic (mystical) thinking, Spinoza's views were judged altogether beyond the pale.

The Great Debate

Here is the debate between Spinoza and the Amsterdam rabbis in the form of an imagined conversation. While no record of their exchange survives, this debate incorporates language from the Writ of Excommunication issued by the Ma'amad, reports about the trial, and excerpts from Spinoza's books. (Italics represent actual quotes from these sources.)

RABBIS: *We have long known of your evil opinions and deeds, and have tried by various ways and promises to turn you from these evil ways.*

SPINOZA: Tell me of what I am accused.

RABBIS: *Daily we receive more information about your abominable heresies,* concerning God, the soul, and the Law.

SPINOZA: *The freedom to philosophize and to say what I think . . . this I want to vindicate completely.*

RABBIS: Is it true that you deny that God creates and rules the world, and say that God and nature are the same, and that God exists only in a philosophical sense?

SPINOZA: *By God's direction I mean the fixed and unchanging order of Nature . . . so it is the same thing whether we say that all things happen according to Nature's law or that they are regulated by God's decree and direction.*

Rabbis: Is it true that you deny that the Torah and the soul are from God?

SPINOZA: I hold that everything comes from Nature *and that the method of interpreting the Torah is no different from the method of interpreting Nature.*

RABBIS: Is it true that you deny that the Jews are God's Chosen People?

SPINOZA: *The individual Jew, taken apart from his social organization and government, possesses no gift of God above other men, and there is no difference between Jew and Gentile. . . . At the present time, therefore, there is absolutely nothing which the Jews can arrogate to themselves beyond other people.*

RABBIS: *You should be excommunicated and expelled from the people of Israel.*

SPINOZA: *I enter gladly on the path that is opened to me, with the consolation that my departure will be more innocent than was the exodus of the early Hebrew from Egypt. This excommunication compels me nothing which I should not have done in any case.*

REASON OR REVELATION?

Spinoza and the Amsterdam rabbis clashed on the core beliefs of Judaism. Although the writ of excommunication did not specify Spinoza's "abominable heresies" we know from his later published works that the philosopher denied almost every major tenet of traditional Jewish belief: that God creates and controls the world, that we can have a personal relationship with God, that God is the source of goodness, that God makes ethical demands upon us, and that the Torah is the revelation of God's will. Spinoza admired some of Scripture but rejected the belief that Moses is God's prophet. He had little use for Judaism's ritual laws and practices (or those of any religion). He rejected the concept of the Jews as the Chosen People.

Modern scholarship has turned up an interesting historical footnote to the excommunication of Spinoza, which seems to verify his denial of Judaism's core precepts. In 1659 (only three years after the excommunication) a monk named Tomas Solano y Robles reported to the Office of the Inquisition in Madrid that he had met Spinoza while in Holland. Spinoza reportedly told the monk that he and another man had been rejected by the Jewish community *"because they thought that the Law was not true, and that the soul dies with the body and that God exists only philosophically, and therefore they were expelled from the synagogue."*

As one of Spinoza's recent biographer's writes:

Spinoza placed all his faith in the powers of reason, his own and ours. He enjoins us to join him in the religion of reason, and promises us some of the same benefits — while firmly denying us others — that traditional religions promise.[1]

Spinoza dared to criticize religion for propagating untruths and fostering dogma and superstitions that led to great evils perpetrated in the name of God. He fervently believed that reason alone could uncover truth, keep our emotions in check, and build an enlightened and tolerant society. Spinoza even argued for a form of secular spirituality — that reason offered personal spiritual bliss:

> *Thus in life it is before all things useful to perfect the understanding, or reason, as far as we can, and in this alone man's highest happiness, or blessedness, consists; indeed blessedness is nothing else but the contentment of spirit, which arises from the intuitive knowledge of God.*[2]

Spinoza was by no means the first Jewish thinker to advocate for reason; the tradition goes all the way back to Philo in the Hellenistic era. But he may well have been the first to insist on the sole employ of reason and the utter exclusion of revelation. Those before him, and many after, shared the goal of a grand synthesis, arguing for reason in the service of revelation. When Maimonides said that *"A man should believe nothing that is not attested (1) by rational proof, as in mathematical science, or (2) by evidence of his senses,"* he was careful to add, *"or (3) by authority of prophets or saints."*

Acknowledgment of the truth of Torah conveyed by Moses is part of Maimonides' definition of core belief for every Jew, and is included in his "Thirteen Principles of Faith."

In explaining the purpose of his most famous philosophical work, *The Guide for the Perplexed*, Maimonides writes:

> *The object of this treatise is to enlighten a religious man who has been trained to believe in the truth of our holy Law . . . and at the same time has been successful in his philosophical duties. Human reason has attracted him to abide within its sphere. . . . If he be guided solely by reason . . . he would consider that he had rejected the fundamental principles of the Law . . . [and] be left with those errors which give rise to fear and anxiety, constant grief and great perplexity.*[3]

Spinoza did not see it that way at all. He thought the truth of reason alone would set us free. He begins his own magnum opus, the *Tractatus*

Theologico-Politicus with the hopeful wish and subtitle: *"Wherein is set forth that freedom of thought and speech not only may, without prejudice to piety and the public peace, be granted; but also may not, without danger to piety and the public piece, be withheld."* He ends his magnum opus on a more cautionary note that the revolution of thinking he is calling for

> *seems exceedingly hard; it may nevertheless be discovered. Needs must it be hard, since it is so seldom found. How would it be possible, if salvation were ready to our hand, and could without labor be found, that it should be by almost all men neglected? But all things excellent are as difficult as they are rare.*[4]

The profound influence of Spinoza on Western philosophy and government can be seen in the political philosophy of John Locke, who in turn influenced the founding fathers of the United States. A remarkable passage from a letter of Thomas Jefferson to his nephew in 1787, just over a century after Spinoza's death, stands as a testament to this exiled Jew's "religion of reason":

> *Shake off all the fears of servile prejudices under which weak minds are servilely crouched. Fix reason firmly in her seat, and call to her tribunal for every fact, every opinion. Question with boldness even the existence of a god because, if there be one, he must more approve of the homage of reason that that of blindfolded fear.*
>
> *You will naturally examine first the religion of your own country. Read the bible then, as you would read Livy or Tacitus . . . those facts in the bible which contradict the laws of nature, must be examined with more care, and under a variety of faces. Here you must recur to the pretensions of the writer to inspiration from god. Examine upon what evidence his pretensions are founded. . . . In fine, I must repeat that you must lay aside all prejudice on both sides, and neither believe nor reject any thing because any other person, or description of persons have rejected or believed it. Your own reason is the only oracle given you by heaven.*[5]

THE BOUNDARIES OF JUDAISM

The Amsterdam Jewish Council felt that it had no choice but to expel Spinoza from its midst. His excommunication came with the warning that *"no one should communicate with him, neither in writing, nor accord him any favor nor stay with him under the same roof nor come within four cubits in his vicinity."* Spinoza's beliefs were deemed to be so beyond the pale of acceptable Judaism that the leaders of the community were apparently afraid that his heresies could cause real harm. They decreed the harsh punishment of totally isolating him, even from family and friends, with the dual hope that his ideas would wither and Spinoza himself would repent.

The case of Spinoza tests the boundaries of Judaism. Exploring these boundaries raises many questions: Is there a limit on freedom of expression within the Jewish community? Are certain philosophical beliefs incompatible with Judaism? Is there such a thing as secular Judaism? Can one separate being Jewish from Judaism, and, for example, claim to be an atheist *and* a Jew? Who is a Jew, and who decides?

If the Amsterdam rabbis and the Ma'amad hoped to silence Spinoza, they failed. For sure, Spinoza was ostracized from his community, and he never returned. Yet Spinoza never converted nor renounced his Jewish identity. He steadfastly maintained his independence from all organized religion. Both the Jewish and Christian religious establishments harshly denounced him, but his reputation only grew with the publication of his books.

As Rebecca Goldstein begins her study of Spinoza:

> By what right is Bendictus Spinoza included in this series, devoted as it is to Jewish themes and thinkers? Can the seventeenth-century rationalist, who produced one of the most ambitious philosophical systems in the history of Western philosophy, be considered, by any stretch of interpretation, a Jewish thinker? Can he even be considered a Jew? Benedictus Spinoza is the greatest philosopher the Jews ever produced, which adds a certain irony to his questionable Jewishness.[6]

Yet Spinoza's challenge helps lay the groundwork for the reform of Judaism (see chapter 9). So too is he an inspiration for a Jewish movement in Europe called the *Haskalah*, which called for the engagement of Judaism with Western culture, and which in turn fostered a movement of Jewish nationalism called Zionism (see chapter 10). Einstein counted himself an admirer of Spinoza, and famously said, *"I believe in Spinoza's God who reveals himself in the orderly harmony of what exists, not in a God who concerns himself with fates and actions of human beings."* Likewise, Israel's founding father and first prime minister, David ben Gurion, openly urged that Spinoza's excommunication be rescinded. (It never was.)

JEWS AND JUDAISM ON TRIAL

The debate over the boundaries of Judaism continues today, more than three centuries after Spinoza. New ideas that threaten the religious establishment are often the subject of vigorous dissent. Like Spinoza, those who embody these radical notions are subject to trials and tribulations.

Perhaps the most prominent example from our time involves Rabbi Mordecai Kaplan, who was raised in a traditional home and became an Orthodox rabbi. Like Spinoza, Kaplan began thinking about God in very new ways. Kaplan began questioning the notion of a supernatural being that intervenes in the world at will, in favor of a naturalistic notion of God, expressed in the highest ideals of human beings. His ideas were articulated in a series of books, most notably *Judaism as a Civilization* (1934), *The Meaning of God in Modern Jewish Religion* (1936), and the *Sabbath Prayer Book* (1945).

For his radical views, Kaplan was subject to the rare but harsh punishment of excommunication. The Union of Orthodox Rabbis in New York expelled Kaplan in 1945, forbid its community to read Kaplan's new prayer book, and is reported to have burned his books. Kaplan went on to become a faculty member at the Jewish Theological

Seminary, the rabbinical school of the Conservative movement. Later he established a new denominational movement in the Jewish community, called Reconstructionist Judaism, which promoted his new ways of looking at Jews and Judaism.

The ongoing debate over identity boundaries led to the famous "Brother Daniel" case in Israel. Brother Daniel was born Oswald Rufeisen in Poland and raised as a Jew. During the Second World War he escaped the Nazis by taking refuge in a Christian convent, and there he converted to Christianity. After the war he became a Carmelite monk and moved to Israel. Brother Daniel applied for Israeli citizenship under the Law of Return, arguing that he was still a Jew. His lawyers argued that under Jewish law, *"a Jew, even if he has sinned, remains a Jew"* (Talmud: Sanhedrin 44a). Opposing lawyers made the case that by the reasonable perspective of the "man in the street," a Jew who converts to another religion cannot reasonably be considered Jewish. In 1958 the Israeli Supreme Court ruled against Brother Daniel's Israeli citizenship as a Jew under the Law of Return. (He eventually did gain citizenship through a much longer naturalization process.)

A final example: In 1994, after a long period of study and debate, the Union for Reform Judaism (URJ) rejected the application of a congregation that called itself "humanistic." The congregation emphasized the cultural heritage of Judaism, and, most controversially, it deleted all references to God in its prayers. While affirming the right of individual Jews to hold such views, the URJ judged the ideology of the congregation to be incompatible with Reform Judaism, ruling:

> *The congregation sees itself as a Jewish group, but its liturgy deletes all mention of God, either in the Hebrew or in English. . . . Their philosophy doesn't admit of either Covenant or commandments. Rabbi Gunther Plaut* [chair of the Central Conference of America Rabbis Responsa committee at the time] *wrote: "Persons of varying shades*

of belief or unbelief, practice or non-practice may belong to [URJ] *congregations as individuals, and we respect their rights. But it is different when they come as a congregation whose declared principles are at fundamental variance with the historic God orientation of Reform Judaism.*[7]

Almost all the questions we ask about Judaism and Jewish identity today have their origin in Spinoza, the prophet of modernity.

9

Geiger and Hirsch and Frankel

Reform or Conserve?
The Debate over Evolution in Religion

Faith and reason . . . is the guarantee for [Judaism's] survival.
ABRAHAM GEIGER

Our slogan is Moderate Reform.
ZECHARIAS FRANKEL

To obliterate the tenets and ordinances of
Judaism — is that the Reform we need?
SAMSON R. HIRSCH

FRIENDS TURNED ADVERSARIES

As Jews became full citizens in Western Europe in the early 19th century, new ideas about Judaism began to emerge. Jews began receiving both a secular and a religious education. They studied philosophy, and Spinoza's challenge of reason loomed large in their thoughts. So too did the pioneering thinking of Moses Mendelssohn, who argued that one must be "a man in the street and a Jew at home," that is, that Jews must end their isolation and engage with the society around them while preserving their unique identity and beliefs.

A grassroots Jewish Reform movement began in Germany when some congregational leaders began instituting changes in the worship service, like the use of the vernacular (prayers in German), eliminating objectionable or redundant prayers, mixed seating, choirs, and formal sermons. These changes elicited fierce opposition from traditionalists, who saw them at best as imitations of Protestantism and at worse as against Jewish law.

Reactions to these reforms would affect the thinking of three leading German rabbis and their relationships with each other. Abraham Geiger,

Samson Raphael Hirsch, and Zecharias Frankel were all contemporaries during this remarkable period of change. They were colleagues, and Geiger and Hirsch were actually friends for a while, in the same city. Yet as time went on they increasingly disagreed with each other on how to respond to the changes in the Jewish world. Each would go on to espouse a distinct ideology, and become in effect the founding fathers of the modern denominations of Judaism we know today.

Abraham Geiger (1810–1874) served as a congregational rabbi in several German cities, and became closely aligned with those advocating for change. He established and organized the first meetings of German rabbis calling for reform. At the same time he immersed himself in scholarly pursuits. In 1872 he founded the Institute for the Scientific Study of Judaism. Geiger advocated for the academic analysis of the Bible and other religious texts. For both his organizational and philosophical efforts he is considered the father of Reform Judaism.

Samson Raphael Hirsch (1808–1888), like Geiger, served a variety of pulpit positions, and developed a friendship with Geiger while they both lived in Bonn. He too devoted time to scholarship. Hirsch authored an influential book called *The Nineteen Letters*, which made the case for retaining traditional belief and practice even while joining in modern society. As such, he is often called the father of modern Orthodox Judaism.

Zecharias Frankel (1801–1875) was born in Prague, educated in Budapest, served in Austria, and then settled in Germany. His career involved a number of disputes with both German authorities and with the organization of Reform rabbis, which he initially joined but later broke away from over the extent of reform. In 1845 he famously stormed out of a rabbinical conference, unable to agree to the elimination of Hebrew for important prayers. In 1854 he was appointed head of the new Jewish Theological Seminary in Breslau, which accepted the new scientific study of Judaism while still considering the texts sacred. For staking out a middle ground position, Frankel is considered the father of Conservative Judaism.

The Great Debate

Here is a debate between Rabbis Geiger, Hirsch, and Frankel in the form of an imagined conversation. All three rabbis knew and conversed with each other, and Geiger did debate Frankel at an 1845 conference. This debate incorporates language from each of the rabbis' sermons and books and the transcript of the conference. (Italics represent actual quotes from these sources.)

GEIGER: *For the love of heaven, how much longer can we continue this deceit, to expound the stories from the Bible from the pulpits over and over again as actual historical happenings, to accept as supernatural events of world import stories which we ourselves have relegated to the realm of legend?*

HIRSCH: Would you deny the Torah? *The very essence of Israel's being rests upon the Torah.*

GEIGER: I do not deny the Torah. But *the treatment of the historical content of the Bible as part of the science of Judaism must be subject to . . . the science of history.* All laws and all prayers that are unworthy or irrelevant should be eliminated.

HIRSCH: *To cut, curtail and obliterate the tenets and ordinances of Judaism — is that the Reform we need? To remodel the Divine service in accordance with the demands of the age — is that the Reform we desire?*

GEIGER: *The course to be taken, my dear fellow, is that of critical study. Judaism need not fear such an unprejudiced critical approach.*

FRANKEL: *Our slogan is Moderate Reform. Time hurries onward and radical reforms are demanded, but we do not want to forget that not all demands of our times are justified. Representation of the total popular will and of science — these are the two main conditions for a reform of Judaism.*

GEIGER: So you agree that both *faith and reason . . . is the guarantee for [Judaism's] survival?*

FRANKEL: I do, but *so much that is characteristic in Judaism has already been obliterated.* For example, *I believe that a part of the service be held in German, [but] Hebrew must predominate. Our youth must be taught Hebrew in order to understand the service and the Bible.*

GEIGER: And you agree that *from now on no distinction between duties for men and women* should be made?

FRANKEL: *When the will of the people is expressed . . . what authority could deny them this right?*

TRADITION OR CHANGE?

In the brave new world of religious freedom and scientific advancement, Rabbis Geiger, Hirsch, and Frankel debated core issues of Jewish belief and ritual. At the heart of their discussion was the nature of revelation. From Spinoza on, some Jews began asking: Is the Torah history or legend? Who wrote the Torah? How should the Torah be studied?

These weighty matters preoccupied the sermons and writings of these leaders during this agitated period of mid nineteenth-century Germany. Overarching these questions is the fundamental quandary: tradition or change? The study of modern science and history was suggesting to scholars that all things change and adapt over time. The equivalent question for the emerging Jewish community in the modern world was: Does this evolution apply to Judaism as well?

Geiger and the other founders of Reform Judaism believed that Judaism has always evolved and should of course continue to change with the times. Their academic study revealed a long process of evolution within both Jewish thought and practice. Their belief in both faith and reason in guiding religious decision-making gave them the authority and confidence to recommend many new changes. In fact, Geiger maintained that the secret to Judaism's success was to adapt to the times, and he called for radical shifts to meet the demands of modernity. Geiger and others from his generation began a reform of Jewish tradition that would radically affect the Jewish community. Reform Judaism in the United States would grow to become the largest Jewish denomination of the largest Jewish community in the world. Moreover, the principles Geiger espoused, from critical study of the Torah to equal treatment of men and women, would be adopted by the majority of modern Jews.

Hirsch and the traditionalists do not believe that Judaism is subject to evolution. The revelation of the Torah by God to Moses contains an unchanging message for all time. Human beings can interpret the Torah, but they cannot change it. Hirsch maintained that the secret to Judaism's success was adhering to the eternal commandments of the Torah. Hirsch did not reject integrating into the modern world (which distinguishes modern Orthodox Judaism from ultra-orthodox Judaism), but he allowed no compromise in traditional belief or practice. From his perspective, Torah-true Judaism is the only authentic Judaism. While a minority of Jews in the United States and Israel consider themselves Orthodox (strictly observing *halakhah,* Jewish law), the traditional community remains strong and influential.

Frankel agreed with Geiger in principle that Judaism must evolve, but much more slowly and cautiously. His slogan was "moderate reform." Later, the Conservative movement he helped found would adopt the motto "tradition *and* change." Frankel's approach has sometimes been called the middle ground, and Conservative Judaism counts almost as many adherents as Reform. Many modern Jews desired change in Jewish ideology and practice, but not a radical break from the past. They sought to maintain traditions to link themselves with the past and were afraid that too much change would result in the loss of Jewish identity.

The persistence of multiple streams, or denominations, in the Jewish community testifies that the debate on evolution in Judaism is alive and well.

REFORMING RITUAL

The pioneers of Reform Judaism introduced sweeping changes into Jewish worship and observance of the lifecycle. In a series of five conferences in Germany from 1844–1871 the following innovations, and even more, were approved:

1. prayer in the vernacular (native language) of the community
2. organ during service
3. choirs in service
4. repetitious and "outdated" prayers eliminated
5. prayer for Messianic Age instead of Messiah
6. riding to synagogue on Shabbat permitted
7. women eligible to serve as witnesses
8. equal rights and responsibilities for women
9. equal (double-ring) ceremony for weddings
10. accepting civil divorce documents
11. mourning customs modified.
12. dietary laws (kashrut) become optional

These ritual changes were the first step in the creation of Reform Judaism. Soon after, Geiger and other thinkers articulated an ideological backing for their changes. The final step was organizational: the establishment of congregational and rabbinic institutions to give shape to a movement.

The first major statement of Reform Judaism in the United States (Pittsburgh Platform, 1875) affirmed all these changes, and went even further, stating:

> *We recognize in the Mosaic legislation a system of training the Jewish people for its mission during its national life in Palestine, and today, we accept as binding only the moral laws and maintain only such ceremonies as elevate and sanctify our lives, but reject all such as are not adapted to the view and habits of modern civilization.*
>
> *We hold that all such Mosaic and Rabbinic laws as regulate diet, priestly purity and dress originated in ages and under the influence of ideas altogether foreign to our present mental and spiritual state. They fail to impress the modern Jew with a spirit of priestly holiness; and their observance in our day is apt rather to obstruct than to further modern spiritual elevation.*[1]

Objections to some of the more dramatic reform gave impetus

to the establishment of the Conservative movement in the United States at the turn of the century. Refusal to accept these innovations solidified the Orthodox movement. In retrospect the debate between three rabbis in Germany 150 years ago was in truth the beginning of an ongoing conversation about what modern Judaism should look like. It was a microcosm of the diversity that characterizes the Jewish community today.

10

Herzl and Wise

A Jewish State?
The Debate over Zionism

The Promised Land . . . where at last we can live as free men
on our own soil and die in peace in our own homeland.
THEODOR HERZL

We are perfectly satisfied with our political and social
position. It makes no difference to us . . . what particular
spot of the earth's surface we occupy.
RABBI ISAAC M. WISE

COMPETING VISIONS

Theodor Herzl (1860–1904) was a young, assimilated Jewish journalist and writer in Vienna when in 1895 he witnessed the trial of Capt. Alfred Dreyfus in France. Dreyfus was accused of treason, and his conviction (eventually overturned) unleashed a torrent of anti-Semitism that included cries of "death to the Jews" at the ceremony where he was stripped of his rank. The event cemented Herzl's conviction that hatred against the Jews would never cease in Europe and that the only hope for the Jewish people was to rebuild their own country in their ancestral homeland. From then on, Herzl worked tirelessly to organize a political movement, Zionism. That same year he completed a book, *Der Judenstaat (The Jewish State)*, laying out his vision. He met with kings, queens, sultans, dukes, rabbis, and Jewish philanthropists in an effort to raise awareness, funds, and political support. Herzl convened the First Zionist Congress in 1897 in Basel, which laid the groundwork for a modern Jewish homeland. Though he died of a heart ailment at only forty-four, Herzl is considered the founding father of political Zionism and a national hero in Israel, where he is buried.

Rabbi Isaac M. Wise (1819–1900), having grown up in Bohemia, Prague, and Vienna, was quite aware of European anti-Semitism. He immigrated to the United States in 1846, first serving pulpits in Albany and Cincinnati. Wise tirelessly devoted himself to building a progressive Reform movement in his adopted country. He established the Hebrew Union College in 1875 to train American rabbis, and soon thereafter founded the Union of American Hebrew Congregations (eventually to be called the Union for Reform Judaism, or URJ). Wise saw an exceedingly bright future for the Jewish community in the United States, and for all his efforts is considered the founding father of American Reform Judaism. The goal of Zionism was to ultimately separate the Jewish people from their surroundings and return them to a Jewish state. The goal of Reform Judaism was to integrate into the society around them while preserving Jewish identity. It is no wonder that Herzl and Wise clashed about whether returning to a Jewish state was the right direction for the Jewish people.

The Great Debate

Here is the debate between Herzl and Wise in the form of an imagined conversation. While there is no evidence that these two men met, they were aware of each other's activities, and Wise mentions Herzl by name. This debate is composed from Herzl's diary and speeches, along with Wise's address to the Central Conference of American Rabbis in 1897.

HERZL: *The Jewish question still exists. It would be foolish to deny it. We have honestly striven everywhere to merge ourselves in the social life of surrounding communities, and to preserve only the faith of our fathers. It has not been permitted to us.*

WISE: *The persecution of the Jews in Russia and Rumania and the anti-Semitic hatred against the Jewish race and religion, as it still exists in Germany, Austria, and partly in France roused among the persecuted and outraged persons the hapless feeling of being hated strangers among hostile Gentiles. [But here] we are perfectly satisfied with our political and social position.*

HERZL: *We are one people — One People! [We need] the Promised Land, where it is all right for us to have hooked noses, black or red beards, and bow legs without being despised for these things alone. Where at last we can live as free men on our own soil and die in peace in our homeland.*

WISE: *It can make no difference to us . . . what particular spot on earth's surface we occupy. We want freedom, equality, justice and equity to reign and govern the community in which we live. All this agitation on the other side of the ocean concerns us very little.*

HERZL: *We are one people — our enemies have made us one without our consent, as repeatedly happens in history. Distress binds us together, and, thus united, we suddenly discover our strength. Yes, we are strong enough to form a State, and indeed, a model State.*

WISE: *[You] revive among certain classes of people the political national sentiment of olden times, and turn the mission of Israel from the province of religion and humanity to the narrow political and national field, where Judaism loses its universal and sanctified ground.*

HERZL: *Zionism is a return to the Jewish fold even before it becomes a return to the Jewish land.*

WISE: *[Zionism] is a momentary inebriation of morbid minds, and a prostitution of Israel's cause to a madman's dance.*

HERZL: *God would not have preserved our people for so long if we did not have another role to play in the history of mankind.*

ETHNICITY OR FAITH?

Underlying Herzl and Wise's impassioned words are two radically differing views of the Jewish people.

Herzl views the Jewish people as an ethnic group. Like other ethnic groups that have a homeland, the Jews deserve a country of their own. Herzl reminds us that *"our enemies have made us one without our consent."* The long history of anti-Semitism proved to Herzl that other people looked upon the Jews as a competing nation, not as fellow citizens. Herzl believed that *"we are strong enough to form a State, and, indeed a model State. We possess all human and material resources necessary for the purpose."* So convinced was Herzl that the Jews needed a country of their own that at one point he was even ready to accept that this state be located in Uganda rather than Israel!

Wise views the Jewish people not as an ethnic group, but as a faith community. He believes that what distinguishes the Jewish people is not a homeland, but religion. At the 1897 conference of Reform rabbis at which he spoke, Wise helped craft a resolution that dramatically makes this point: *"Resolved, that we totally disapprove of any attempt for the establishment of a Jewish State. Such attempts show a misunderstanding of Israel's mission. . . . We reaffirm that the object of Judaism is not political nor national, but spiritual."* Wise goes on to say that the Jewish people's task is to promote the highest values of its religion: peace, justice, and love, to the whole world.[1]

When Rabbi Wise went on record opposing Zionism, he was reflecting the majority view of many early Reform rabbis. In the Pittsburgh Platform of 1875, considered the first major statement of the American Reform Movement, we find these strong words: *"We consider ourselves no longer a nation, but a religious community, and therefore expect neither a return to Palestine . . . nor the restoration of any of the laws concerning the Jewish state."* It is important to note that the Reform movement was by no means the only segment of the Jewish community against Zionism. Similar nineteenth-century statements can be found among the Orthodox and the secular.[2]

WHEN HISTORY INTERVENES

The Zionist idea faced relentless opposition in its first decades for the very ideological reasons expressed in the Herzl-Wise exchange. Yet the Zionists gained momentum, fueled by the power of their idea and by continued anti-Semitism. Prominent Reform rabbis like Stephen Wise and Abba Hillel Silver began to speak in favor of a Jewish state. As the storm clouds of Nazi Germany gathered, the Reform movement essentially repudiated its previous stance in the Columbus Platform of 1937. It now proclaimed: *"In the rehabilitation of Palestine, the land hallowed by memories and hopes, we behold the promise of renewed life for many of our brethren. We affirm the obligation of all Jewry to aid in its up-building as a Jewish homeland."*

Theodor Herzl was on the right side of history, while Rabbi Wise was on the wrong one. Little could these men have known in 1897 what the twentieth century would bring. The Holocaust essentially settled the debate about the need for a modern Jewish state that would serve as both refuge and reviver of a decimated people.

Herzl, despite fighting a monumental battle that left him discouraged and exhausted, had an inkling that in the long run the power of his idea would prevail and his dream would be realized. He wrote in his diary, in a passage that has now become famous: *"At Basel I founded the Jewish State. If I said this aloud today, I would be answered by universal laughter. Perhaps in five years, and certainly in fifty, everyone will know it."* Indeed, the modern State of Israel came into being precisely five decades later.

Jews around the world hailed the establishment of the State of Israel in 1948 as a modern miracle and quite possibly the greatest moment in Jewish history. Almost everyone in the Jewish community became a Zionist. The Reform movement's San Francisco Platform of 1976 acknowledged that:

We are privileged to live in an extraordinary time, one in which a third Jewish commonwealth has been established in our people's ancient

homeland. We are bound to that land and to the newly reborn State
of Israel by innumerable religious and ethnic ties.

ZIONISM TODAY

While supporting the basic right of Israel to exist as a Jewish State is
no longer in dispute in the mainstream Jewish community, the exact
meaning of being a Zionist remains open to debate. For example, the
San Francisco Platform that acclaimed our ties to Israel went on to state:

*We encourage aliyah for those who wish to find maximum personal
fulfillment in the cause of Zion. At the same time that we consider the
State of Israel vital to the welfare of Judaism everywhere, we reaffirm
the mandate of our tradition to create strong Jewish communities
wherever we live. A genuine Jewish life is possible in any land.*

Not long after Israel's establishment, Prime Minister David Ben Gurion
conducted a well-publicized debate with a prominent American Jewish leader named Jacob Blaustein. Ben Gurion, espousing a view that
is often termed "classical Zionism," argued that all Jews now had the
responsibility to move to Israel. At the very least he insisted that all
Jews owe loyalty to the Jewish state. Blaustein, reflecting the perspective of the San Francisco Platform, which represented the majority
of America Jewry, demurred. Blaustein noted that while American
Jews should offer support Israel, as American citizens they must give
allegiance only to the United States.

Questions also arise about whether someone who calls him- or
herself a Zionist should always support policies of the Israel government. In the vital democracy that is Israel citizens of the Jewish
state often disagree among themselves. For example, one of the most
intense ongoing debates within Israel is whether Israel should evacu-
ate settlements in the West Bank to create a Palestinian state. Zionists
wrestle not only with when they should disagree with the government
of Israel, but how. In the case of American Jews, or all others that live

outside Israel, is it acceptable to publicly criticize the government of Israel from afar? Or does being a Zionist mean disputes should be kept in the family and only expressed privately?

While the essential question of Zionism may not be a matter of debate today, an entire array of issues relating to the Jewish state remains controversial.

Afterword

Debate and disputation are not only encouraged within Judaism, they are at the heart of Jewish history and theology. As such, I believe that a chronicle of great debates, like those presented in this book, is central to understanding the history of Jewish ideas. I wrote this slim volume as an introduction (an invitation, really) to an intellectual history of Judaism conveyed through the art of argumentation.

Beyond their historical importance, what makes these disputations so compelling is that nearly all the great Jewish debates, regardless of when they took place, are *still being argued.* Chapter by chapter I endeavor to demonstrate that rather than being a series of *resolved* arguments, Judaism is, in effect, an accumulation of *unresolved* arguments!

We come to the realization that many of the debates continue in some form to this day. The questions remain relevant; the controversies are still alive. This is the dialectical nature of Jewish thought and Judaism's secret strength. In the spirit of Abraham and his descendents, I urge you to question without inhibition and to debate without intimidation. Seek out those opportunities with a measure of "holy hutzpah" . . . so long as your argument is for the sake of heaven!

Notes

INTRODUCTION

1. Samson Raphael Hirsch, *Commentary on Pirkei Avot (5:20)*, as quoted in Jewish Theological Seminary Torah Commentary, June 10, 2010.

2. Or Rose, *Tikkun* (Nov.-Dec. 2008): 64; commenting on Rabbi Nachman of Bratslav in *Likkutei Moharan*, p. 54.

3. Clifford Librach, "Dissent from the Dissenters," *CCAR Journal* (Summer 2010): 41.

1. ABRAHAM AND GOD

1. Elie Wiesel, *A Jew Today* (New York: Random House, 1978), p. 6.

2. As related by Samuel Dresner. See *Levi Yitzhak* (Bridgeport CT: Hartman House, 1974), pp. 86–87. These and other tales are also presented in Anson Laytner, *Arguing with God* (Northvale NJ: Jason Aronson, 1990).

3. As related by Mitchell Bard in "Britannica Blog," March 5, 2009, www.britannica.com/blogs.

2. MOSES AND KORAH

1. Yeshayahu Leibowitz, on "Parashat Korah," in *Weekly Parasha* (New York: Chemed, 1990), p. 143.

2. Martin Buber, *Moses: The Revelation and the Covenant* (New York: Harper and Row, 1958), pp. 189–90.

3. Shlomo Riskin, as cited in Torah column, *Jerusalem Post*, July 1, 1989.

4. Harold Schulweis, as cited in Torah column, *Jerusalem Report*, July 10, 1997.

5. Evan Wolkenstein, as cited in Torah column, *American Jewish World Service*, June 28, 2008.

6. Bradley Artzon, as cited in Torah column, *Bat Kol Institute*, June 27, 2008.

3. THE FIVE DAUGHTERS AND THE TWELVE TRIBES

1. Gunther Plaut, *The Torah: A Modern Commentary* (New York: Union for American Hebrew Congregations, 1981), p. 1218.

2. Abraham Geiger and colleagues, as cited in *The Rise of Reform Judaism* (New York: World Union for Progressive Judaism), pp. 253–55.

4. DAVID AND NATHAN

1. Abraham Joshua Heschel interview with Carl Stern, transcript from *Eternal Light* television broadcast, 1973.

6. HILLEL AND SHAMMAI

1. Joseph Telushkin, *Hillel: If Not Now, When?* (New York: Nextbook/Schocken, 2009), p. 84.

2. Telushkin, *Hillel*, p. 89.

7. THE VILNA GAON AND THE BAAL SHEM TOV

1. Attributed to the Ba'al Shem Tov, as cited in Yitzhak Buxbaum, *The Light and Fire of the Baal Shem Tov* (New York: Continuum, 2005), pp. 244–45. The source for the story is said to be *Ikkarei Emunah*, Lodz edition, 1933, pp. 9–23.

2. Buxbaum, *The Light and Fire of the Baal Shem Tov*, p. 248.

8. SPINOZA AND THE AMSTERDAM RABBIS

1. Rebecca Goldstein, *Betraying Spinoza* (New York: Nextbook/Schocken, 2006), p. 11, citing *The Ethics IV*, appendix IV.

2. Goldstein, *Betraying Spinoza*, p. 236.

3. Sherwin Nuland, *Maimonides* (New York: Nextbook/Schocken, 2005), p. 137.

4. Baruch Spinoza, *Tractatus Theologico-Politicus*, as cited in Goldstein, *Betraying Spinoza*, p. 257.

5. Thomas Jefferson letter of August 10, 1787, to his nephew Peter Carr, as cited in Goldstein, *Betraying Spinoza*, p. 261.

6. Goldstein, *Betraying Spinoza*, p. 3.

7. As related by Elyse Frishman in URJ Torah column online, May 25, 2009.

9. GEIGER AND HIRSCH AND FRANKEL

1. All texts relating to the Reform rabbinical conferences in Germany and the United States can be found in Gunther Plaut, *The Rise of Reform Judaism* and *The Growth of Reform Judaism* (New York: World Union for Progressive Judaism, 1963).

10. HERZL AND WISE

1. Central Conference of American Rabbis yearbook, 1897.

2. Plaut, *Rise of Reform Judaism* and *Growth of Reform Judaism*. Texts relating to Zionism can be found in Arthur Hertzberg, *The Zionist Idea* (Philadelphia: Jewish Publication Society, 1959).

Room for Debate

Questions for Reflection and Discussion

CHAPTER 1. ABRAHAM AND GOD

The Text: Genesis 18:22–32

1. Does "the Judge of all the earth deal justly" in the Genesis account?
2. Does Abraham have the right to question God?
3. Does Abraham win this debate, or does God?

Contemporary Issues

1. When is collective punishment morally acceptable?
2. Was the collective punishment of the Japanese by the dropping of atomic bombs on Hiroshima and Nagasaki justified?
3. Are civilians who aid terrorists innocent and deserving of noncombatant immunity?

CHAPTER 2. MOSES AND KORAH

The Text: Numbers 16:1–16

1. Should Moses have been willing to listen to Korah?
2. Does Korah have a case, that all are holy?
3. Were Korah and his followers legitimate dissenters?

Contemporary Issues

1. Is Jerusalem a holy city, and subject to political negotiation?
2. Is the Sabbath holy, and requiring cessation from work?
3. Is the Bible holy, and God's word?

CHAPTER 3. THE FIVE DAUGHTERS AND THE TWELVE TRIBES

The Text: Numbers 27:1–11, 36:1–12

1. Is the compromise of women inheriting but marrying within the tribe a good one?
2. Are women second-class citizens under biblical law?
3. Can the *halakhah* regarding the traditional role of women be categorized as separate but equal?

Contemporary Issues

1. Is the inclusion and equality of women in Judaism complete today?
2. Should gays be extended all religious rights in Judaism, including marriage?
3. Are illegal immigrants the equivalent of the biblical "stranger" and justified in receiving a path to full citizenship?

CHAPTER 4. DAVID AND NATHAN

The Text: 2 Samuel 11–12

1. Should David have been allowed to remain king?
2. Does the punishment fit the crime?
3. Does David repent?

Contemporary Issues

1. What examples of prophetic figures speaking "truth to power" exist today?
2. Does this story have parallels to the impeachments of Richard Nixon and Bill Clinton?
3. Should immoral orders from superiors be refused?

CHAPTER 5. BEN ZAKKAI AND THE ZEALOTS

The Text: Gittin 56a-b, Avot d'Rabbi Natan 4:5

1. Was accommodation — or resistance — to Rome in the national interest?
2. Does anything justify Abba Sikra's actions against his fellow citizens?
3. Is there a middle ground between pacifism and armed resistance?

Contemporary Issues

1. Should Masada be a symbol of heroism today?
2. Should the United States support armed resistance against dictators?
3. Should Israel negotiate with sworn terrorist organizations?

CHAPTER 6. HILLEL AND SHAMMAI

The Text: Shabbat 21b, 31a; Ketubot 16b

1. Is Shammai's attitude toward a prospective convert understandable?
2. Should a bride be flattered even if it involves a lie?
3. Doesn't it make more sense to light the Hanukkah candles Shammai's way?

Contemporary Issues

1. Should a greater effort be made to welcome interfaith couples into Jewish life?
2. Should the Jewish community make a greater effort to gain converts?
3. Should a qualified judge be denied a nomination based on judicial philosophy?

CHAPTER 7. THE VILNA GAON AND THE BAAL SHEM TOV

The Text: Various attributed quotes

1. Is prayer — or study — the primary means of relating to God?
2. Does excessive celebration lead people away from Torah?
3. Is "every spoken word" a message from God?

Contemporary Issues

1. Should Jewish prayer today be traditional or innovative?
2. Should it include chanting, meditation, folk singing, dancing?
3. What is the most appropriate metaphor for God: parent or ruler?

CHAPTER 8. SPINOZA AND THE AMSTERDAM RABBIS

The Text: Writ of Excommunication and Spinoza writings

1. What, exactly, are Spinoza's "evil opinions and abominable heresies"?
2. Are they worthy of excommunication?
3. Was Spinoza an atheist?

Contemporary Issues

1. Should Judaism today be based on reason or revelation?
2. Should the humanistic congregation have been admitted to the Reform movement?
3. Should Brother Daniel have been given citizenship under the Law of Return?

CHAPTER 9. GEIGER AND HIRSCH AND FRANKEL

The Text: Rabbis' sermons, books, and conference transcripts

1. Can the laws of the Torah change with the times?
2. Should Jewish prayer be all or part in Hebrew, or in the vernacular?
3. Should the Torah be subject to modern historical analysis?

Contemporary Issues

1. Is patrilineal descent (Judaism determined through the father) legitimate?
2. Should kashrut be eliminated, or modified to be more ethically responsible?
3. Is a civil divorce sufficient for a Jewish couple?

CHAPTER 10. HERZL AND WISE

The Text: Herzl diary and speeches; Wise address to the CCAR

1. Are the Jewish people a faith community or an ethnic group?
2. Is a Jewish homeland the only real answer to anti-Semitism?
3. Why was Wise so vehement in his opposition to Zionism?

Contemporary Issues

1. Can Jewish life flourish again in Germany and the former Soviet Union?
2. Should all Jews be Zionist, in the sense of supporting Israel?
3. Do Jews outside Israel have a right to criticize the government of Israel?

Further Debate

Recommended Reading

One might expect that many if not all of Judaism's great debates presented in this volume have been the subject of their own book-length treatment. Yet this is not the case. And, although some of the debates have received scholarly attention in articles or chapters of larger works, none have been written as they are presented here. Below are primarily popular but reputable biographies of the main characters of these debates, along with excerpts from writings, remarks, and speeches that will be of interest to readers. Most of these are contemporary works, but some reach back to older studies because they are classics or remain the only references available.

CHAPTER 1. ABRAHAM AND GOD

Feiler, Bruce. *Abraham: A Journey to the Heart of Three Faiths.* New York: HarperCollins, 2002.

Rosenblatt, Naomi. *Wrestling with Angels.* New York: Delacorte, 1995.

Dershowitz, Alan. *The Genesis of Justice.* New York: Warner, 2000.

CHAPTER 2. MOSES AND KORAH

Kirsch, Jonathan. *Moses: A Life.* New York: Ballantine, 1999.

Milgrom, Jacob. *The JPS Torah Commentary: Numbers.* Philadelphia: Jewish Publication Society, 1990.

Fields, Harvey. *A Torah Commentary for Our Times.* New York: UAHC, 1990.

CHAPTER 3. THE FIVE DAUGHTERS AND THE TWELVE TRIBES

Cherry, Shai. *Torah Through Time.* Philadelphia: Jewish Publication Society, 2001.

Plaut, Gunther. *The Torah: A Modern Commentary.* New York: UAHC, 1981.

Etz Hayim: Torah and Commentary. New York: Rabbinical Assembly, 2001.

CHAPTER 4. DAVID AND NATHAN

Pinsky, Robert. *The Life of David.* New York: Nextbook/Schocken, 2008.

Kirsch, Jonathan. *King David.* New York: Ballantine, 2001.

McKenzie, Steven L. *King David: A Biography.* New York: Oxford University Press, 2000.

CHAPTER 5. BEN ZAKKAI AND THE ZEALOTS

Neusner, Jacob. *A Life of Yochanan ben Zakkai.* Leiden: Brill, 1970.

Neusner, Jacob. *First Century Judaism in Crisis.* New York: Ktav, 1982.

CHAPTER 6. HILLEL AND SHAMMAI

Telushkin, Joseph. *Hillel: If Not Now, When?* New York: Nextbook/Schocken, 2010.

Buxbaum, Yitzhak. *The Life and Teaching of Hillel.* Lanham MD: Roman & Littlefield, 2008.

Glatzer, Nachum. *Hillel the Elder.* Washington DC: B'nai B'rith, 1957.

CHAPTER 7. THE VILNA GAON AND THE BAAL SHEM TOV

Buxbaum, Yitzhak. *The Light and Fire of the Baal Shem Tov.* New York: Continuum, 2005.

Ben-Amos, Dan, and Jerome R. Mintz. *In Praise of the Baal Shem Tov.* New York: Schocken, 1984.

Etkes, Immanuel. *The Gaon of Vilna.* Los Angeles: University of California Press, 2002.

CHAPTER 8. SPINOZA AND THE AMSTERDAM RABBIS

Goldstein, Rebecca. *Betraying Spinoza.* New York: Nextbook/Schocken, 2006.

Nadler, Steven. *Spinoza: A Life.* New York: Cambridge University Press, 2001.

Nadler, Steven. *Rembrandt's Jews.* Chicago: University of Chicago Press, 2003.

CHAPTER 9. GEIGER AND HIRSCH AND FRANKEL

Weiner, Max. *Abraham Geiger and Liberal Judaism.* Philadelphia: Jewish Publication Society, 1962.

Plaut, Gunther. *The Rise of Reform Judaism.* New York: WUPJ, 1963.

Myers, Michael. *Responses to Modernity.* New York: Oxford University Press, 1990.

CHAPTER 10. HERZL AND WISE

Elon, Amos. *Herzl.* New York: Holt, Reinhart, and Winston, 1975.

Hertzberg, Arthur. *The Zionist Idea.* Philadelphia: Jewish Publication Society, 1959.

Plaut, Gunther. *The Growth of Reform Judaism.* New York: WUPJ, 1963.